The ORATORY PROJECT

The **ORATORY** PROJECT

Matt Eventoff

THE ORATORY PROJECT

Editing: **Yasmin Sara**
Cover Design: **Christy Bui**
Interior Design: **Christy Bui**
Proofreading: **Deborah Emmitt**

ISBN Paperback: 978-0-578-86764-9

Printed in the United States of America

Speak With Style
BOOKS

To the greatest wife, mother, father, sister, nieces, puppy, and family a man could ever hope to be blessed with.

To my mentors, old and new, thank you for being a part of my journey.

To my mentees, friends, and other "teachers" who teach me how to be a better version of me every day, thank you.

To the next-generation orators who will forever change this world for the better through communication, go get it!

And to anyone who thinks that their voice doesn't matter, it does. Very much. Use it.

Contents

PART 2: Strategies

Introduction

Years have passed since I released *Oratore: The Art of Communication* and the speed and ferocity with which technology has transformed communication since then is like no other time in modern history. Never before have individuals faced so many often conflicting messages on a minute-by-minute basis.

We have more information available to us at any moment in time than history's most powerful leaders could access in a week. Social media apps surface news faster than any multinational news organization ever could. Users upload more video content in a day than all major U.S. television networks created over the past century.[1] And as a result, we are inundated with non-stop emails and texts.

At the same time, our attention span is shrinking. Microsoft's Insight team estimated that a consumer's average attention span is eight seconds—a full second shorter than that of a goldfish.[2] It may be more difficult than ever to create a memorable presentation with a message that will resonate long after one sees or hears it. How many times have you sat through a conference or class with very little recollection of the message behind some of the presentations you literally *just* saw?

While the mediums we use to communicate are evolving, many of the fundamentals of effective communication remain

---

1 O'Neill, Megan. "Longest YouTube Video Ever Will Take You 23 Days To Watch." *Adweek*, Adweek, 28 July 2011, www.adweek.com/digital/longest-youtube-video/.

2 McSpadden, Kevin. "Science: You Now Have a Shorter Attention Span Than a Goldfish." *Time*, Time, 14 May 2015, www.time.com/3858309/attention-spans-goldfish/.

unchanged since the days of Demosthenes, Aristotle, Cicero and the well-known rhetoricians of Ancient Greece.

This book draws from those greats as well as contemporary rhetoricians—from Malala to Mandela to Muhammad Ali—to give a toolkit to be a master communicator in the 21st century. In these pages, I will share with you some of the tips and methods I've collected by studying the greats, and by coaching athletes, executives, and politicians on communication over the last two decades. These are methods that helped Cicero overcome his fear of public speaking, Muhammad Ali find his voice, and Lincoln shorten his prose. You will also find tips on how to handle communicating in today's fast-paced and ever-changing technologically advanced world. I hope these tips will help you become a more confident, eloquent, and powerful communicator, as they have for me.

If you've ever faced an audience with sweaty palms, you're not alone. If you've wondered how to become a better communicator during meetings or a group project, or struggled with putting your best foot forward in a job interview, then this book was created for you.

What this book *is not designed to do* is make you a better communicator simply by reading it.

A master communicator is not born. Effective communication must be practiced, and it will help you in every facet of life. You don't become a master communicator by simply reading a book. Rather, a great communicator studies, practices, and prepares.

The Oratory Project is intended to offer suggestions, techniques, and advice—some of which may be beneficial to you. However, in order for communication to be effective, it must be authentic. While some techniques here might work for 90% of the population, they might not work for you. Discard those that don't and utilize those that do.

But how do you determine what works and what doesn't?

I rely on the advice of a master in his own field, legendary martial artist Bruce Lee: "Adapt what is useful, reject what is useless, and add what is specifically your own."

PART 1

Core

I turn pale at the outset of a speech and quake in every limb and in all my soul.

Cicero

CHAPTER 1

Fear

Glossophobia, the fear of public speaking, is consistently rated as one of people's top fears. If you are nervous or anxious before a presentation, YOU ARE NOT ALONE! Many, many people have faced this same anxiety (including Sir Winston Churchill, Aristotle, Mahatma Gandhi, Demosthenes, and President Lincoln).

You may be saying to yourself, "Okay, Eventoff, that's fine, but having me relate my anxiety to orators of the past is a little tough to imagine, as I can't see (or, other than Churchill, hear) any of them." Fair enough. Let's turn to today. Are you the only person who experiences the fear of public speaking? Not even close. How about Prince Harry? Warren Buffett? Adele? All had anxiety prior to speaking in public at some point in their careers. It doesn't matter how famous you are, how wealthy you are, or how successful you are. From Demosthenes to Gandhi, many of the most famous orators of all time have felt the same angst.

In this chapter, I'm going to provide you with three tools to help you overcome these nerves: the illusion of transparency, plateauing and reframing nervous energy, and visualization. I have seen these strategies work for anyone from professional athletes, to C-suite executives, to movie stars. Backed by the best and most recent scholarly research, these tools worked for them, and they'll work for you.

No One Can See You Sweat: The Illusion of Transparency

> "I know they are watching me tremble and sweat!"
>
> "Can they see me shake?"
>
> "I get so blotchy when I am nervous and I know that the audience can tell!"

A common, recurring misconception is that the audience can perceive just how anxious and nervous you are. That they are judging you. That your physiological responses to stress (trembling, sweating, shaking) are apparent to everyone.

This perception is simply untrue, and it is also very detrimental. When you think the audience can see how anxious you are, the result is always the same: an increased stress response.

> My head was reeling, and I felt as though the whole court was doing likewise.
>
> **Mahatma Gandhi, 1889**
> (as a young lawyer)

I have worked with thousands of speakers over the years and know that you are always more nervous than you appear. Having coached and prepared speakers across the globe, I've found that no matter the culture, religion, context, or audience, this is a universal principle. You may appear nervous, and the audience may see bits of sweat, but you never appear to be as nervous you feel. The audience is not in tune with your emotional state.

A study by Dr. Kenneth Savitsky and Dr. Thomas Gilovich, from Cornell University's Department of Psychology, confirms this point.[3] Savitsky and Gilovich had participants deliver impromptu speeches in pairs. After each individual spoke for three minutes, the speaker was asked to rate him- or herself in terms of how nervous the speaker thought he or she appeared, and how nervous the other speaker appeared.

The results were striking: speakers systematically overestimate how nervous they appear to others. In Savitsky and Gilovich's words, "When individuals are called to speak in public, they do not appear as nervous as they think they do."

This is attributed to a well-documented psychological effect called the "illusion of transparency"—the illusion that a person's emotional or mental state is as obvious to others as it is to that individual. You are typically not quite as open a book as you may think.

But there's more. In the second part of the study, they found that ". . . public speakers are often nervous over the (largely illusory) prospect that their nervousness is apparent to their audience—a concern that serves, ironically, to increase their nervousness."

Let that sink in. Thinking that others see you are nervous (even when they don't) makes you more nervous. It increases your stress response, boosting your anxiety even further. Savitsky and Gilovich call this "the cycle of nervousness."

On top of that, Savitsky and Gilovich conducted a follow-up study where the design of the first was replicated, pairing off participants giving impromptu speeches. This time, however, they explained the illusion of transparency, telling the participants that their nervousness is not as apparent as they would

---

3 Savitsky, Kenneth, and Thomas Gilovich. "The Illusion of Transparency and the Alleviation of Speech Anxiety." *Journal of Experimental Social Psychology*, vol. 39, no. 6, 2003, pp. 618–625, https://doi.org/10.1016/s0022-1031(03)00056-8.

think. Participants who were informed about the illusion of transparency delivered speeches that were ranked more highly, and they were perceived as less nervous.

By learning about the illusion of transparency, speakers were able to escape the cycle of nervousness. Knowing that you do not appear as nervous as you think you do makes you a better speaker.

In the 1980s, an advertising campaign for Dry Idea, an anti-perspirant, told millions of people to "Never let them see you sweat." When it comes to public speaking, don't worry—they won't see you sweat.

Fear of Public Speaking: Reframing Fear

You step up on stage. Your palms sweat, your pupils dilate, your heart rate increases. You start taking deeper, faster breaths.

> The only thing we have to fear is fear itself.
>
> **President Franklin D. Roosevelt**

Whether you have ever played an organized sport or acted in a school play, you'll recognize these signs. In any instance, physiologically and biologically, they are identical.

Take the engine from between your ears out of the equation and everything else is the same, whether you're excited for the basketball game or fearful because you're going to speak. Your stomach drops, internal organs stop, digestion stops. The blood rushes from your extremities, your vision narrows and your pupils dilate. This is your body preparing you to focus on what's at hand.

Most individuals associate these responses with anxiety or nerves in a negative way. In reality, they are part of your body's mechanism to help you achieve peak performance.

And that is a good thing.

That's right—it's a good thing.

Contrary to popular thought, nervous energy and the physiological responses that follow, properly channeled, will make for a more impactful presenter and presentation.

One of the keys to channeling this nervous energy successfully is to understand what is actually happening when our acute stress response, or "fight or flight" response, kicks in.

Dr. Jeremy Jamieson, an expert on social stress and Professor of Psychology at the University of Rochester, has extensively studied how stress impacts individuals in relation to risk, decision-making, and performance.

> "The problem is that we think all stress is bad. Before speaking in public, people often interpret stress sensations, like butterflies in the stomach, as a warning that something bad is about to happen.
>
> But those feelings just mean that our body is preparing to address a demanding situation. The body is marshaling resources, pumping more blood to our major muscle groups, and delivering more oxygen to our brains. Our body's reaction to social stress is the same flight or fight response we produce when confronting physical danger. These physiological responses help us perform, whether we're facing a bear in the forest or a critical audience."

Professor Jamieson conducted a study in conjunction with Harvard University that showed the effects of understanding and channeling our nervous energy when public speaking. He prepped one group on the science of our body's physiological response before delivering a speech to a panel of judges, while the other group acted as a control, receiving no training. The prepped group was able to channel their physiological response, pumping more blood through the body per minute and scoring significantly higher on their speeches than the other participants. Even those who self-reported as experiencing significant social anxiety still outperformed their non-anxious, unprepared counterparts.

Simply understanding the body's natural response when stress is initiated has a positive effect on how individuals view and address anxiety prior to presenting. Individuals tend to no longer look to eliminate their anxiety, and instead try to manage and plateau it to keep it from becoming all-consuming.

Jamieson's study proved the same thing I've seen in clients for decades: understanding how and why your body is responding to fear allows you to channel nervous energy and perform at a higher level. This is reframing our body's physiological response, turning the response to anxiety into improving performance.

"Reframing" in and of itself is not a new concept, but reframing the stress response through the psychological and biological response as it relates to public speaking is new, exciting, and extremely powerful.

Visualization

Musicians, professional athletes, and actors use the power of visualization to help them to succeed. Violinists imagine placing each of their fingers in the right position on their fingerboard for an upcoming performance. Soccer players do the same thing before approaching the ball on a free-kick. They imagine where and how they'll hit the ball, visualize it curling around the "wall" of defenders, and picture the ball sailing into the net. Broadway actors visualize themselves recalling their precise lines in the precise position to the delight of their audience.

Athletes, musicians, and actors have been running through upcoming important events in their minds, visualizing every detail and a successful outcome for centuries. They credit visualization with reducing apprehension and higher achievement.

Professor Joe Ayres from Washington University found that the power of visualization increases public-speaking success as well.[4] He found that just one fifteen-minute visualization session significantly improved audience-rated performance and decreased speaker-reported anxiety. Interestingly, the more detail in which a speaker visualized their speech—some went as far as picturing their shoes—the more effective their visualizations were.

You can use visualization to rehearse your speech in your mind. Don't only imagine yourself delivering the speech, but visualize the audience reacting with excitement and interest.

Let's try an exercise now. Think of an upcoming speaking engagement as you read the section below:

> As I begin warming up for the speech, I notice the weather conditions around me. I am feeling anxious and know that when I perform well, I am usually feeling like this. I feel the heat building, I feel my adrenaline pumping, and I know it's a great thing. This is how I feel right before I am at my best. This is how every NBA or EPL

---

4 Ayres, Joe, and Tim Hopf. "Visualization: Reducing speech anxiety and enhancing performance." *Communication Reports* 5.1 (1992): 1-10.

star feels before taking the field. How every performer feels before taking the stage.

I am PUMPED. I start to think about my goal for the speech. I think about the open. I tell myself I am going to nail this, in a big way. I have the open down. I have worked toward this goal and am ready to go. As I walk toward the room, I start to feel increasingly aware of my surroundings, as my heartbeat quickens and breath deepens. And then I start to feel excitement build, because I know this is a good thing. I do a few neck rolls and some isometric exercises. I feel my muscles tense and loosen.

I am here, and I wouldn't want to be anywhere else. I feel like a champion. I have earned this. I feel the air in my lungs and I look out at the audience ... I see a few faces back. I see smiles. I see people who aren't yet aware of how good this is going to be. I see some folks looking at their phones. I am excited. There is only one face that matters, and it is mine. I've worked hard for this moment. My eyes narrow as I look at the folks in the front row. I have practiced and prepared and I am in a good place. I feel anxious, but I feel good. I feel right.

I feel like I feel before I win. I feel like I feel before I am incredibly excited! I feel like I feel when it is a great day! It smells like it smells when I have a great day! The air feels like it feels when it's a great day! My mouth is dry, just like it is before anything great I have ever done. Today is My Day. My Day!

Twenty-Three Tips and Strategies to Overcome Fear

Right now you are likely saying to yourself, "Okay, now I know that no one can see how nervous I am, and that the physical and emotional stress of speaking is similar to that of my last basketball game. While that's all well and good, I'm still nervous."

That's where you should be.

The previous ideas help, but they're only theoretical. Here are twenty-three strategies you can put into practice to help you reframe your fear and deliver a great speech or presentation:

1. **Prepare.** The more prepared you are, and the more familiar you are with the material you are presenting, the better the presentation will be.

2. **Practice.** Once you have prepared, you MUST practice. Practice early and practice often. Rumor has it that Sir Winston Churchill practiced one hour for every minute of speech content he was delivering. Thus, a five-minute presentation is equal to five hours of practice. How long do you spend practicing?

3. **Check out the room.** In this case, familiarity breeds comfort. Surprises on the day of a presentation are not fun and can increase anxiety tenfold. Check out your environment ahead of time. Is there a podium that you will be standing behind? What technology will you be using, and how does it work?

4. **Read the room.** While it's not always an option, when you have the opportunity to meet a few audience members beforehand, take it! Arrive ten minutes early and introduce

yourself to a few people. If you are presenting mid-day, arrive before a key break to meet a few folks.

5. **"Seed" the audience.** Ask friends, associates, or colleagues to come and hear you speak. Talk to the conference organizers when you arrive so you know a few people before you begin your presentation. Locate where familiar faces are sitting before you take the stage. If anxiety starts to build, focus on these friendly faces. They'll provide a calm and cooling force that will allow you to collect yourself.

6. **The audience is on your side.** Nine times out of ten, the audience is rooting for you to succeed, not wanting you to fail or fall flat. The audience is there to hear what you have to say. Assume they are excited about your speech or presentation.

7. **Listen to music.** If you watch a live boxing match, MMA competition, or NFL pregame show, you'll likely see world-class athletes in the locker room listening to music. Listening to music helps athletes get in the zone, eliminate distractions, chase away anxiety or negative thoughts, and get pumped up and excited. This technique also works really well prior to public speaking. So, invest in some quality headphones, and throw on your favorite song before you go on stage. Listening to music beforehand can be a presenter's best friend.

8. **Body movement.** A few minutes before taking the stage, "waggle" your jaw (lateral movement), bend forward and dangle your arms and let them shake, shake your hands over your head, and utilize simple stretches that require no equipment other than your body weight and a fixed structure you can press against (such as a wall), or a locked door that you can pull against—just not too hard! We are not trying to break

down muscle, we are simply trying to redirect energy. All of these movements, when incorporated with proper breathing, can warm your body, relax your mind, and calm your nerves.

9. **Body movement, part II.** As a former amateur boxer, nothing personally prepares me more for public speaking than light shadow boxing a few minutes before I go on. I know a CEO who (literally) does twenty push-ups prior to every earnings call. Focused movement helps even more than generic movement because it tends to take your thought process in a different direction. For a boxer, shadow boxing is focused movement. Tai Chi is focused movement. Yoga is focused movement. Walking up and down a staircase while counting is focused movement. While shadow boxing may look like a person just throwing random punches, it is anything but. A boxer actually sees or visualizes an opponent, and every punch, feint, or movement is based around what the invisible opponent is doing.

10. **Standing sit-ups.** Constricting the abdominal wall may reduce the level of epinephrine in bloodstream (a hormone associated with the fight or flight response, also known as adrenaline). I have found the most effective way to utilize this approach prior to speaking is to "crunch" and release the abdominal muscles while standing (lying down and doing sit-ups is probably not optimal in presentation attire!). To me, the physical sensation in your abdomen is very similar, if not the same, as when you laugh—which is probably as effective but would result in many more stares if done while seated in an audience. I use this constantly, even as I am approaching the podium, and I find it to be very effective.

11. **Put the pressure elsewhere.** The more interactive your presentation, the less pressure you will feel as the presentation starts to flow like a conversation. Most people are much more comfortable in a conversation than in delivering a formal presentation.

12. **Stay caffeine free.** It is best to avoid copious amounts of caffeine on presentation day due to the stimulant's increase of epinephrine and the fight or flight response. Avoid salty foods to avoid drying out your mouth as well. I also tend to eat lighter on the day of a presentation, as this keeps me feeling sharp.

13. **Utilize water breaks.** A properly placed water bottle and well-timed break in the presentation to take a sip not only gives the presenter a break for a few seconds, but it can also be an effective technique to "reset" the audience.

14. **Work on your open.** The first minute of the presentation is usually when your tension will peak. Having a well-prepared, effective, and engaging opening will lessen anxiety dramatically.

15. **The restroom.** Don't laugh—on presentation day, the restroom is your ally. Ten or fifteen minutes before presenting, head to the restroom to allow yourself the opportunity to breathe, listen to inspirational music, close your eyes, get into your zone, and, of course, use the bathroom. If called upon to do a last-minute presentation, you will always be able to steal five minutes in the restroom. Use it to pull yourself together and relax.

16. **Anxiety . . . interrupted.** When you are less than five minutes from taking the stage, the anxiety is starting to build,

your heart is pounding, and you keep telling yourself to calm down. One of my favorite techniques is to pick a random number over 1,000 and start counting backwards. Another technique is to count by multiples such as sevens, nines, or elevens. These exercises aren't easy, allowing for thought interruption, essentially halting the building of anxiety.

17. **Anxiety . . . distracted.** Maybe you are not a math wizard, or the number technique is not effective for you. So instead, try mentally reciting the alphabet backwards. This is another way to achieve thought-process disruption, leaving you more relaxed and less anxious.

18. **Breathing exercise #1: Belly.** Try taking three deep belly breaths (which sounds like what it is). Slowly inhale through the nose for a count of five to fifteen seconds (fifteen is optimal). Meanwhile, keep one hand on your diaphragm and feel it enlarge as you inhale. Hold for five to ten seconds and then exhale through your mouth slowly (or nose, if you are sitting in an audience and don't want to exhale through your mouth) again for a count of five to fifteen seconds (fifteen is optimal). Repeat three times. This breathing technique is a great exercise to do a few minutes before you are going to speak.

19. **Breathing exercise #2: Ujjayi.** Also known as oceanic breathing, Ujjayi breathing is remarkable. It is a yogic breathing technique that I first learned about while struggling through Vinyasa yoga classes. It is similar to deep belly breathing, however, this time, the mouth stays closed throughout the entirety of the exercise. Take a deep, slow breath in through your nose, hold your breath for a moment, and then direct your breath out against the back of

your throat, still through your nose. It is often referred to as oceanic breathing, as the sound your breath makes on the exhalation is reminiscent of gentle ocean waves (or perhaps a serene Darth Vader).[5]

20. **Breathing exercise #3: Alternate nostril (my personal favorite).** All you need for this is your thumb, your pinkie finger, and your nose. To begin, simply cover your left nostril with your left thumb, then slowly and deeply inhale for five seconds to start (ten is optimal).

    Then, immediately cover your right nostril with your left pinkie finger, while keeping your left nostril pressed closed. You'll want to make sure your mouth is closed at all times during this exercise, so, at this point, you are essentially holding your breath.

    Again, hold for five seconds (ten is optimal). Then, remove your left pinkie from your right nostril and slowly exhale for a five to ten second count. Wait two seconds and repeat the same technique, instead inhaling through your left nostril as you hold your thumb on your right nostril to keep it closed—hence the name "alternate nostril breathing." The Sanskrit name of this technique is *nadi shodhana*, or "purifying channel," and I learned this from one of my first yoga teachers twenty years ago. While it might seem complicated the first few times, with practice, it becomes easier relatively quickly. I find that daily practice for even one minute is incredibly beneficial, and that the more often one practices, the calmer one becomes when using this technique. In my experience, another really neat aspect of this exercise is that once you

---

5 Miller, Tim. "What Is Ujjayi?" *Yoga Journal*, 28 Aug. 2007, www.yogajournal.com/practice/what-is-ujjayi/.

have really practiced it and made it a habit, you can use it to bring a sense of calm much more quickly.[6]

21. **Use notes.** Memorization + anxiety = poor performance. Take the anxiety of memorization away by using an index card with key bullet points to help you stay on track. This removes the pressure of remembering what to say and the order in which to say it. Without worrying about memorization, your mind can stay clear and in the moment.

22. **Mantra.** Athletes and many executives use a phrase, or "mantra," as a technique to focus attention and energy. My mantra is pretty basic—I consistently repeat, over and over, both mentally and even (very softly) verbally, "It's go time. My time. Go time." Athletes use phrases like "no fear" or "no pain" or "let's go!" constantly. Why? They work. One of my favorites comes from Scott Jurek. For those not familiar with Scott, he is an ultra-marathoner, which means he runs races that are often over a hundred miles. His mantra of choice is, "This is what you came for." I encourage you to try one from an athlete you like, or you can create your own. The most important thing is to try it and see if it works for you.

23. **Scaling.** There is one last technique that I frequently suggest to people who've had a traumatic public-speaking experience in the past, called scaling. After a traumatic experience, your memory tends to exaggerate how poorly the event went. The more time that goes by without that thought pattern being interrupted, the bigger the event feels, and in this case, the more anxious you will feel prior to your next presentation.

---

6 If you get stuck, there are many good videos on YouTube that can help. Here's an example of one: https://youtu.be/ONMwbQETrYI

> It's critical to break this pattern. This is done through scaling—finding low-stakes presentation opportunities and slowly, over a period of time, scaling up by taking those opportunities while increasing audience size and presentation "stakes."

There are a number of other techniques that I have heard about over the years that many people have found to be effective. These include utilizing acupuncture points, looking at pictures of loved ones prior to presenting, squeezing objects like stress balls or tennis balls to create comfort. These are just some examples, perhaps you have heard of or used others. Try as many as possible—the important part is to *see what works for you*.

So the next time you are about to present, do yourself a favor. Take a deep breath, and picture Sir Winston Churchill or Abraham Lincoln. They are two of the greatest orators ever, and both suffered from a fear of public speaking. And this isn't just true for political players and world leaders.

Think about major Hollywood actors and actresses who also suffer from glossophobia. It is a long list, and it seems that every month, a new famous personality takes to a talk show, Instagram story, or a YouTube video to express the debilitating fear or angst he or she faces before speaking publicly. And these are folks who perform in front of thousands of people on a constant basis. That's right! It's not just you! In fact, while I can't speak conclusively for all of humanity, I am comfortable going so far as to say that you are in the majority.

You are not alone! I can promise you that if you incorporate much of what you just read, your next presentation will feel (and be) significantly better.

CHAPTER 2

Development

Why present at all? Is it simply to transmit information? Judging by the offices filled with unseen PowerPoint presentations, the inboxes filled with thousands of unread emails, the conference calls occurring where participants are having in-office meetings at the same time, and the conference audiences who are focusing on something else while a speaker is presenting, it would appear that we have enough information to last many lifetimes.

Message is everything. Without a message, there is no real reason to communicate. The core of creating a successful presentation lies in the identification and development of a message. Once you have the message, then what? You need a way to deliver it! That's where structure comes in. There are a number of effective structures to utilize, depending on the presentation. I'll outline my favorites in this chapter.

After you craft a message and the structure of your presentation, how are you going to get anyone to listen to you? We've all sat through too many presentations that we forgot immediately upon leaving the room. What are you going to do in that first eight seconds before your audience decides to check their stocks/email/texts/TikTok? We need to convince our audience to listen and we need to capture their attention. That's where the open comes in.

Now we have a solid message, a great structure, and a powerful open. How do we ensure that the audience leaves as interested as when you opened? The close! Psychology studies have shown that people judge an experience largely based on how they feel at the end[7]—and a powerful closing is the perfect time to hammer home your message.

So now that your presentation is bookended with a strong open and close, and it has a structurally sound message, how do you connect the dots to keep the audience interested throughout? This is where transitions and an engaging delivery come in. But if your audience is still tuning out, how do you re-engage them, and if necessary, even end early? If you're wondering what the answers could be, read on.

What Is Your Message?

The first step in creating audience interest is to determine why the audience should be interested, which helps define your message. You shouldn't communicate simply to relay information. That is a waste of time to both the presenter and the audience! The purpose of public presentation is to compel the audience to feel something, to think about something, to be curious about something, to do something.

A message is not simply the regurgitation of information "because, well, my boss/friend/colleague/spouse said I need to share the information." In all of these instances, there is still a reason *why* you need to share the information. Identifying that reason will go a long way in helping you to shape your message.

7 Studies led by Barbara Fredrickson and Nobel prize winner Daniel Kahneman provided ample evidence that people judge experiences largely based on their peak experience and how they felt at the conclusion. This psychological heuristic underscores how important it is to have a particularly memorable moment and a strong conclusion during any talk.

In my experience teaching thousands of individuals over six continents and eighty countries, here is the best definition I've found for a message:

The message is the essence of why you are communicating.

Every presentation has a message. Unfortunately, it usually goes undiscovered. If you try to communicate too many things, you end up communicating nothing. So how do we develop a message that anyone and everyone can understand? The following tips can help.

First and foremost, every message should be:

Relevant: Does it matter to the audience?
Relatable: Can one relate based on previous experience?
Retainable: Is it impactful enough to have staying power?
Repeatable: Is it memorable and easy to repeat (conceptually)?

Asking yourself the following **four questions** will help you formulate exactly why you are communicating at all, and it will also result in your message achieving the guidelines above. Remember, a presentation is not about the presenter; it is always about the audience. These questions will help you sit in an audience member's seat.

1. **What** are you trying to accomplish?
2. **Who** is your audience?
3. **What** is the one thing that they absolutely need to know?
4. **Why** should your audience care?

Answering the first two questions will establish the baseline of what you are presenting—both the material and its context.

The last two questions (What and Why) are the focus, as they are the crux of developing a message. Your audience may very well forget much of your presentation. Consider: What can you not afford for them to forget?

What: If my audience only remembers one thing that I say, what should that be?
Why: Why *should* my audience care? Not why *do* they care . . . because the truth is, they may not. Your job as a presenter is to educate them about why your topic matters to them.

Combining these two answers will result in your message.

However, making **a bold claim with no backup** will leave an audience unconvinced. Telling someone why they must care about something and then not supporting that statement will lead to confusion.

Provide three points that bring substance to your message. Further **substantiate and support** each of those three points with backup information, including material listed below.

- Simple Stories
- Facts
- Figures
- Quotes
- Statistics
- Contrasts
- Questions (rhetorical or literal)
- Metaphors (something is something): "All the world's a stage"
- Similes (something is *like* something or *as* something): "Strong as an ox"
- Anecdotes
- Analogies
- Comparisons

- Contrasts (contrasting pairs)
- Testimonials
- Literature
- Social Proof
- Research
- Studies
- Opinion
- Media Coverage
- Historical Precedent
- Market Success
- Industry Measures
- Examples

Finally . . . Ask yourself **one last question.**

What do you want the audience to do?

If your audience were to walk away differently than they walked in, what would you want that difference to be? How do you want them to respond to your message? Often resulting in a call-to-action, your answer here will help you to shape your message.

Examples of Presentation Structures

Now that we've honed a message, let's continue talking about structure.

CLASSIC STRUCTURE

This is the most common structure, and I find it to be most effective for the majority of presentations, whether they're five or forty-five minutes long. This structure is pliable and malleable, and it can be easily implemented. I have used this structure to introduce a key message, support it, bring it to a conclusion, allow a short break for an audience to reset (sometimes as short as fifteen to twenty seconds, sometimes as long as five minutes) and then begin with a fresh open and a fresh presentation. I find this to be much more effective than trying to introduce multiple messages into one longer presentation.

- **Open:** Draw the audience in
- **Message:** Immediately then to the "message," the crux of the presentation
- One to three key points, all of which are supported (with transitions)
- **Close:** Create interest in hearing more and creating memorability

SOLUTION STRUCTURE

An effective structure when solving a problem or introducing a solution to a problem an audience may not yet know they are facing.

- **Open:** Frame the problem
- **Fact:** To support the existence of the problem ("Nine in ten Americans don't know . . .")
- A few points about why it matters
- **Close:** Solve the problem

DEBATE STRUCTURE

This structure is tricky but effective, and demands complete transparency. One MUST introduce every possible argument against his or her own solution—and solve them. Leaving out any legitimate argument renders this structure useless.

- **Open:** Frame the issue
- Give each argument against your point (without prejudice) and with full benefit
- Take time (and great care) to explain why each argument is incorrect. In other words, poke a hole in each argument you have laid out
- Finish with your solution after all other options have been exhausted
- **Close:** Call-to-action

THREE ACT STRUCTURE (THINK MOVIES)

- **Open:** Set up by setting the stage
- **Confrontation:** This can be an internal confrontation; does not have to be between individuals
- **Close:** Resolution

PROFESSOR MONROE'S MOTIVATING SEQUENCE

Professor Alan Monroe, a Purdue University professor of speech in the 1930s, is credited with creating the Monroe Motivating Sequence, a persuasive speech structure that is still widely taught today.[8]

- **Attention:** Grab attention (Open)
- **Need:** Demonstrate a problem or need
- **Satisfaction:** Propose your solution
- **Visualization:** WIIFA (What's In It For the Audience)
- **Action:** Prompt to take action – Problem/solution (Close)

PERSUASIVE SPEECH

This is simply a more exhaustive example of the basic persuasive structure to provide an example and template for usage.

- **Open:** Start strong

  "Be Sincere. Be Brief. Be Seated." ~ President Franklin D. Roosevelt

- **Message:** State it (What + Why = Message)

  "Brevity is the key to effective communication, and the key to more compelling presentations."

8 A fun (and totally irrelevant) fact: The author of this book was born on the Purdue University campus.

- **Transition:** Shift

  "Why is brevity so important?"

- **Support #1:** Statistic

  Lloyd's Attention Span Study
  Dr. Medina's Research

- **Transition:** Shift

  "Now that we have looked at attention span, let's take a look at history."

- **Support #2:** Fact; Anecdote

  "Lincoln's Gettysburg Address was 272 words. 200 of those were one-syllable words and the whole speech was under three minutes.

  Edwin Everett's address, the main speech on that day in Gettysburg, was more than 13,000 words and lasted over two hours. How many remember what Edwin Everett said that day?"

- **Transition:** Shift

  "Now ask yourself, when was the last time you watched a presentation and said, 'Wow, I wish that went on for another thirty minutes!'"

- **Support #3:** Example; Experience

  "Having watched thousands of speeches and presentations, when I overhear people talking during breaks, very, very rarely does anyone talk about the 'riveting past hour.'

This is not a new concept. Cicero (107–43 B.C.), the famous Roman orator (amongst many other professions), stated: 'Brevity is the best recommendation of speech, whether in a senator or an orator.'

There is a misconception that forcing TMI (too much information) and CUA[9] (constant useless acronyms) on an audience is necessary. Remember, if your audience doesn't follow you, or if your audience loses interest, who did you actually influence, persuade, or move?"

- **Transition:** Shift

"So which model of speech will you follow?"

- **Seek support:** Close

"The question really is: who is your presentation designed for, and whose interest is paramount: the presenter or the audience?"

STRUCTURE FOR LONGER PRESENTATIONS (HINT . . . IT'S THE SAME!)

- **Open:** Start strong
- **State it:** Key message/Position/Theme

Now, think of each support as its own mini-presentation, with a brief open and close, and a break for a few seconds in between to allow the audience to digest and re-engage. I tend to prefer utilizing questions as a tool to open these mini-modules, answer with the support, and close by reinforcing the support and/or

9 This may be my favorite CUA.

transitioning. This is an example of what is described above as linking presentations together.

- **Support #1:** Open, Support, Close
- **Support #2:** Open, Support, Close
- **Support #3:** Open, Support, Close
- **Seek Support:** Close the entire presentation

IMPROMPTU SPEECH STRUCTURE #1: PPF

These are structures to use when you have to give a speech with no time to prepare, especially when honoring someone or making a toast.

The following is a widely used technique for dealing with an impromptu invitation to introduce someone, toast someone, or "say a few words" about an organization or an event.

- **Past:** "I have known _________ for . . ."
- **Present:** "Today, I am thrilled to see _________ . . ."
- **Future:** "Wishing _________ a world of happiness . . ."

IMPROMPTU SPEECH STRUCTURE #2: QAC

- **Question:** "Why does ABC need to worry about DEF?"
- **Answer/Message:** "DEF keeps me up at night because . . ."
- **Close:** "Let's follow the counsel of _________, when she stated . . ."

IMPROMPTU SPEECH STRUCTURE #3: PYA

This technique is my personal favorite, as it is the recipe for any effective message. If there is one thing I need you to remember, if you forget everything else I say, what is it? Why should you care? What can you do? What do I want you to do?

- **Point:** "If you only remember one thing that I tell you, I want you to remember _______."
- **Why it matters to you:** "__________ matters to you because . . ."
- **Action:** "So now you should go out and _________."

> Additional tips to deal with impromptu opportunities or opportunities with very short notice:
>
> - Answer the traditional who, what, when, where, why, and how.
> - Start by asking and answering your own question.
> - Make it personal. Address any experience you have had with the topic at hand. If you have no experience, transition by comparing it to a situation you are familiar with.

Strategies for Opening a Presentation

The audience is seated. The lights dim and the room quiets. All eyes are on the dais, waiting for the presentation to begin. All too often, this is what is heard:

> *"Hi, thank you for having me. It is an honor to be here with you today. My name is _________, and I am going to be speaking to you today about _________."*

Looking around, here is what I see:

- People reviewing a physical copy of the program, their previous notes, or additional handouts.

- T-U-T/T-O-T: Typing under table/typing on table. The smartphones are out in full force. It is not unusual to see people engrossed in their laptops, phones, or tablets.
- Eyes looking up. Eyes looking down.
- Eyes looking everywhere but at the speaker.

With all of this going on, how do you effectively open a speech or presentation? Here are twenty-three effective ways:

1. **Quote.** Name any topic and, more often than not, there is a great quote or saying that suits your subject matter perfectly. Here is an example of a quote that I often use to open a presentation on public speaking:

   "It usually takes me more than three weeks to prepare a good impromptu speech." ~ Mark Twain

2. **What if.** Using a "what if . . ." scenario to draw your audience into your presentation's importance early on can work wonders. Encourage your audience to get involved right away by painting a picture of the scenario.

3. **Imagine.** This follows the same thought process as "what if." Put your audience directly into the presentation by allowing each member to visualize a scenario.

4. **Question** (rhetorical or literal). When someone is presented with a question (whether an answer is called for or not), that person intuitively answers it, even if it's just in his or her mind. And guess what? Now that person is involved.

5. **Power word.** The emphasis is on choosing a word or phrase that is compelling (and emphasized).

   "Conflict" (long pause)

"Never again" (long pause)

6. **Triads.** Friends, Romans, countrymen; students, parents, alumni; employees, management, ownership. This should be used with caution, but if delivered cleverly and authentically, it is effective.

7. **Repetition.** "I will not, I will not, I will not . . . give up."

8. **Statement.** A powerful statement, followed by a pause can be very effective. Inspirational political speeches and locker-room speeches often start this way.

   "We cannot win. We can't win."

   (Pause)

   "That's what every newspaper in the country is saying . . ."

9. **Silence.** Yes, silence! A pause, whether two seconds or twenty, allows your audience to sit and quiet down. Most audiences expect a speaker to begin immediately. An extra pause brings all attention right where you want it—on you!

10. **Statistic/Citing research.** Don't use a boring or complicated statistic. Instead, focus on a surprisingly powerful or personalized one.

    "Look to your left. Now look to your right. One of your seatmates will ______."

    "In this room, over 90% of us are going to ______."

    "The size of ______ football fields . . ."

    "The size of New York and Belgium combined . . ."

    "Picture a ______."

11. **Story.** We tell stories every single day. However, it is only when we think consciously about telling a story that our minds go blank. Here are two easy templates to help create a story quickly:

WWWCR	or	TRIPLE C
Who		Character
What		Conflict
Where		Comeback
Conflict		
Resolution		

12. **Current event.** Pick up a *USA Today* a few days before an event, or, in the worst-case scenario, the day of. There will always be an idea to relate to.

    "This morning in *USA Today* we saw that . . ."

13. **Moment in time.** "Just yesterday . . . Last week . . ."

14. **Provocative statement.** Say something attention-grabbing. Again, this should be used with caution. Provocation that arouses curiosity in an audience member is effective. Provocation that insults or offends an audience member is a presentation killer.

15. **Analogies.** "Just as a sword is the weapon of a warrior, a pen is the weapon of a writer."

16. **Five senses.** "It felt like . . . It smelled like . . . It looked like . . . It sounded like . . . It tasted like . . ." (E.g. home-baked chocolate cookies convey warmth; the smell of lemon is clean; warm lavender walls give a sense of calm.) Use visual

language and incorporate other senses to set the scene. I find this to be very effective, as the verbal description can help to paint a visual picture in the mind of an audience member.

17. **Illustrations.** "Picture a _______. It was a perfect summer day . . . salt in the ear, the sounds of seagulls and waves crashing. The ocean was a pallid blue . . ." Again, very similar to using the five senses technique above by verbally creating a visual.

18. **Simile.** X and Y are compared using "like" or "as."

    As blind as a bat

    To work like a dog

    As strong as an ox

19. **Metaphor.** Applying X to Y when it is not literally applicable. Similar to a statement such as:

    Has a heart of gold

    Food for thought

    Time is money

20. **Activity/Movement.** Get them active; get them to do something! Get up. Move. Write something down. Shake hands with the person next to them. Or greet the person behind them. Have them repeat something to you.

    Learning is accentuated when someone needs to actually do something, so here's a neat way to incorporate that into a speech:

    "Repeat after me."

    Or have them draw something in the air:

"Take your index finger and draw a …"

This helps your audience with retention!

21. **Prop.** Props can be used to illustrate a point or begin a story. Care needs to be taken to ensure that the "prop" is not a pen that one waves around or a laser pointer that one clicks repeatedly. A prop could be something that leads directly into an introduction. I have used a bottle of water, a trophy (that was received by someone else!) and a backpack, all introduced with some semblance of this:

    "You might be asking yourselves, 'Why am I standing in front of you with a _____? This _____ actually has everything to do with (subject). *Why?* you might ask.'"

    I then lead into the subject areas. In the three cases listed above, the water bottle is used for a discussion around pollution; the trophy is used for discussion around winning (and why winning has NOTHING to do with trophies), and a backpack is used for a discussion around international travel for weeks on end.

22. **Promise.** "By the end of this presentation, I guarantee that _____." "If we go and do _____, I can promise that _____."

23. **Ask.** Ask the audience to think of something. For example:

    "Think of three times when you were really, really nervous. Think about how that felt. What do you remember most?"

    This is a great way to connect with the audience and also lead into a personal anecdote or bit of research.

One technique that I've left out here is humor. I am not a big fan of preplanned humor or jokes to begin a presentation. While I have witnessed it done very well and effectively, on many, many more occasions I have seen it derail a presenter and lead to a disastrous presentation. One bad joke causes the audience to withdraw and the speaker to lose focus.

Tips on Transitions

Now that you've successfully captured your audience's attention, you need to keep it. One of the most difficult parts of that is how you *transition* between "message supports" and "thoughts" within your presentation. Here are some of the best ways I have found to transition:

- **Questions:** A favorite. "So why would we _________? We would _________ because _________."
- **Chronological:** "First . . ."
- **Markers:** "We established earlier _________. Remember . . ."
- **Itemize:** "Three points . . . a) ________ b) ________ c) ________"
- **Physical:** "Now let's look at . . ." or "We've covered . . ."
- **Adverbs:** While, Often, Recently, Now
- **Phrases:** "Let's look at . . ."

Tips for Closing a Presentation

The moment of truth has arrived. You had them entranced from the start. The audience has been clearly focused, nodding as you delivered your message; eyes locked as you wove through a carefully crafted medley of stories, anecdotes, and analogies, all supporting your mission.

There is no question that the majority of your audience probably agree with what you are saying. Now empowered, the time has come for you to conclude, at which point you exclaim:

> *"In conclusion, I appreciate you giving your time to hear about ______. Thank you."*

And then . . . nothing happens. Everyone quietly claps or just nods, and then leaves the auditorium or conference room.

This is particularly damaging because of those studies that show that people judge an experience largely based on how they feel at its end. What can you do to prevent this from occurring?

Each of the twenty-three tips listed earlier in this section on opening a presentation also work for closing. However, to try something different, here are eleven tried-and-true techniques for closing a presentation:

1. **Offer a direct call-to-action.** A speech or presentation without a clear call-to-action is one that is probably not worth giving. While it may not be appropriate for every speech, there is no clearer way to prompt action than a direct call-to-action.

> "In order to guarantee that we save _____ tomorrow, we need to _____ today. If every person in this room leaves and immediately _____, I can guarantee it will result in _____ next year!"

2. **(Very) Short story/Anecdote.** Show, don't tell! Use a brief story or anecdote to drive the message home. I once had a Major League Baseball player as a client, and he very effectively told the following (abridged) story to end a presentation about teamwork:

   "So, Coach entered the locker room after a pretty tough game in which a number of us had standout performances, and the result was ... a big loss. One of our players went four for four. Coach called him by his last name, Smith, asked him to come up front, and then asked him to stand with the back of his uniform facing the rest of the players. Then he asked a kid who had just been called up from the minors, Jones, to do the same thing. He then said, 'Smith, Jones, I want you to turn around.' When they did, he pointed to the front of the uniform and reminded us all: 'You play for the name on the front of the jersey (the team) not the name on the back (your own).'"

3. **Call-to-question.** It is often very effective to end a presentation or speech with a rhetorical question that captures the message and leaves the audience thinking—especially one that directly ties in a call-to-action:

   "What choice will you make when you leave here today? Will you _____ or will you go about your normal routine?"

4. **Contrast.** One of my favorites! This one is even more effective when tied directly to the closing call-to-action:

   "We can have _____ or we can have _____. The choice is ours, and is based entirely on the decision we each individually make today. ______ or ______. I know I'm choosing ______."

5. **Callback.** Most common.

 "Earlier today ..."

 "As we discussed at the beginning ..."

 "Tying everything together ..."

6. **Steve Jobs close.** One More Thing.

 "One more thing ... In the immortal words of Steve Jobs ..."

7. **Repetition.** Repeating earlier key phrase, and silence (bowed head) . . . then . . . "Thank you."

8. **Powerful phrase.** For example, "Be kind."

9. **Lyrics.** Song lyrics that are powerful:

 "I'm starting with the man in the mirror, I'm asking him to change his ways. And no message could have been any clearer. If you want to make the world a better place, take a look at yourself and make a change."

 ~ "Man in the Mirror" by Michael Jackson

 "If you've lost your way I will keep you safe." ~ Westlife

10. **Quiet.** Have you ever noticed how Broadway shows or concerts end with silence? The spotlight comes on . . . or just quiet, and then after a long pause . . . "Thank you."

11. **Excerpts from literature.** I happen to like John Steinbeck (especially *Grapes of Wrath*).

"Wherever you can look—wherever there's a fight, so hungry people can eat, I'll be there. Wherever there's a cop beatin' up a guy, I'll be there." ~ Tom Joad, *The Grapes of Wrath*

Four Ways to Present a Speech

There are a number of ways to present. I will go over a few here.

1. **Reading.** Done incorrectly, this is a recipe to tune an audience out, whether looking down to read or reading every word on a slide. There is an effective way to read, and that is through the use of rhymeless, meterless verse. See below.

2. **Memorization.** I am a firm believer that memorization is ineffective, and for many reasons. The main reason is that it prevents a presenter from being present, as he or she will always be recalling back for information. I also believe that it causes undue stress on presenters, as forgetting a sentence or a word can throw off an entire presentation.

3. **Notes with bullet points.** This is the technique I favor. Here is a big, deep, heavy secret for any presenter: your audience has no idea of the details of what you are presenting, and unless you are the president and your speech is made public and distributed, no one will ever know if you miss something. I tend to write every speech out long form, using the techniques above to develop message, structure, points, etc. I then practice and practice, slowly culling my presentation down to key bullet points, which I keep on numbered note cards (in the event that I drop them).

4. **Slides as guides.** See Chapter 6 for PowerPoint tips.

READING

So what does rhymeless, meterless verse look like? When I am delivering a presentation or remarks not from notes but from prepared text, I want to ensure that I can deliver it while maximizing eye contact and focusing on my audience. Paragraph form is simply too hard to look at and still maintain flow with your audience. Try reading aloud the following paragraph:

> *To write a speech in verse is not easy, but everyone can do it. It takes a lot of hard work and practice. In the end, it will make your presentation more effective.*

See? It's not easy to read the paragraph and maintain eye contact.

Here is an example in verse (borrowing from William Shakespeare and one of the most famous fictional speeches of all time) with my own "code" so that I can maintain presence with my audience while not missing a beat (P = pregnant pause):

> To be (P) … or not to be … (P)
>
> … THAT *is* the question …
>
> Whether 'tis nobler in the mind …
>
> to suffer …
>
> … the slings and arrows of outrageous fortune (P)
>
> Or … to take arms …
>
> … against a sea of troubles(!)

Another neat technique is staggering. Here is an example:

One can also write

In a staggered form

to allow for easier chunking.

Chunking is the ability

To take a small section of a sentence

And present it while maintaining presence

with an audience

Audience Participation

In any presentation, one of the keys to audience participation is to establish a connection with members of the audience. Remember, they are the reason you are presenting in the first place! This is something I firmly believe you can do even before you begin to formally present.

A presentation doesn't begin when the presenter starts speaking, takes the stage, or even reaches the front of the room. A presentation begins the first time an audience member encounters the speaker. This can be used to your benefit the next time you speak.

How does this work? Introduce yourself before your presentation is scheduled to begin.

"Hi, I'm Matt Eventoff. It is a pleasure to meet you."

Whether speaking to thirty or three hundred people, I try to arrive as early as possible and position myself at the entrance of the room where I am presenting so I can introduce myself. If that isn't possible, and I am already in the room, I try to meet a few people surrounding me. This changes the mood in the room immediately, as I am no longer speaking to a room full of strangers. There are now at least a few friendly faces, and a few folks whom I can count on to participate. And participation typically begets participation.

Re-engaging Your Audience

Let's say your presentation or lecture opened really well. Your message was well prepared, well delivered, and well supported. Your audience was engaged, the nonverbal feedback you received was energizing, and there was a lot of learning going on.

But, now you have reached the ten-minute mark of your presentation and you are beginning to see some yawns. Heads are starting to be supported by fists. Eyes are glazing over. Posture goes from straight up and alert to slumping. Oh no!

You still have a number of points to hit! And, the information coming up is even more interesting. Why are they fading? And how do you get them back?

First, it's important to understand that you may never know why they are fading. It's more important to know how you can get your audience back. How do you keep the level of interest going?

While never a guarantee, here are a few strategies you can use to re-engage your audience:

1. **Ask questions.** The old failsafe. These questions should not be confrontational, probing, or personal. Ask basic questions that no one would find threatening to help to re-engage some of the audience members.

2. **Move around.** Step into the crowd. Leave the lectern behind. Step off the podium. The closer you get to your audience, the more re-engaged some of the audience members become.

3. **Demonstrate.** Demonstrating a concept while literally in the audience can be a powerful technique to re-engage people quickly. You can also ask for a volunteer from the audience to help demonstrate something.

4. **Self-deprecating humor.** Again, I am not a big fan of starting a presentation with a joke or humor. It can go wrong much too easily. That being said, if during your presentation you lightly make fun of yourself and make the audience laugh, you will certainly get their attention. Some people advise against this because you don't want to raise questions about your confidence or credibility. However, if you make fun of yourself and it's something unrelated to the subject of expertise, you can get a few chuckles and re-engage the audience.

5. **Move the audience around.** Get the audience to do something, anything. Move over one chair, stand up, or close their eyes. It just has to be non-confrontational, relevant to your topic, not too intimidating, and not singling out any one individual. Movement raises the energy level. Have them pick up a pen and write something down or draw something.

There are many ways to re-engage or re-energize an audience, but when you are in a tight situation, these techniques are quite effective.

THE EMERGENCY EXIT: WHY EVERY SPEECH NEEDS TWO ENDINGS

The scenario: You have toiled for hours upon hours preparing for your thirty-minute conference speech. You have scripted your presentation to the letter, have practiced it repeatedly, have battled the butterflies and angst in your gut—and the moment of truth is approaching.

But now, the conference organizer is also approaching . . .

He informs you that while you were scheduled to be the final speaker, there is now another speaker after you, and your thirty minutes has become fifteen.

Panic sets in. How can you trim a thirty-minute presentation in half at such short notice? How can you convert a scripted speech in mere moments?

The answer: Emergency Exits.

When it comes to scripted, formal speeches, two endings are often better than one. Having an "emergency exit" prepared will allow you to adapt to a situation such as this, so you can still convey your message to the audience without attempting either to cram thirty minutes worth of information into half that time or to leave out material on the fly.

And this is not the only scenario. It happens more often than most presenters think.

I recently attended a global gala with thousands of attendees and not one, but two, keynote presenters. Both presenters were subject matter experts. They both had clear messaging. Both effectively used rhetorical tools, powerful stories, and personal anecdotes. Both received thunderous applause in the beginning.

And then both kept on going. And going. And going.

What happened next?

People started having quiet conversations, which grew increasingly louder and more overt. Eye rolls. Early exits. Texting.

Conversations after the presentations focused on length rather than content.

Why did this happen?

When one has a prepared text and has toiled for hours on end crafting each word, one also tends to grow more attached to each word.

When this long-winded speech is combined with the acute stress response (fear!), a hall with thousands of attendees, and blinding lights in a presenter's eyes, it becomes very, very difficult to interact with an audience, and even more difficult to focus on the presenter-audience dynamic. That dynamic is often the difference between a memorable message and a bored audience.

Add to all of those stressors a script that doesn't have emergency exits, and a presentation can lose its impact by the second.

So how does one battle this?

The formula is the creation of an Emergency Exit—a paragraph or line you have prepared that would be able to fit in multiple locations throughout your speech, allowing you to be more present and leave the audience craving more rather than getting tired.

It can be a sentence or restatement of your message to be utilized if you sense the audience has grown restless. Often it is a shorter, more concise version of the closing you have scripted. Again, the key is that it can fit in multiple places so you can make an emergency exit if you intuit from your audience that it is time to conclude, or if your time is cut.

I have written quite a bit about a personal preference for bullet points rather than formal scripts, with one reason being the ability to be more "present" with your audience. Understanding that sometimes a scripted presentation may be preferable to the presenter, or even required, whether used or not, the "emergency exit" will allow you to be more present, and therefore more impactful.

As a presenter, of course, you hope not to have to use an emergency exit. Your message is likely important to you, and you want to share that in its entirety with others. In order to do so, an important message requires a well-developed presentation. Hopefully, the techniques and suggestions given in this chapter will prove useful in doing just that, from identifying the message behind your talk, to engaging the audience throughout, and to driving them to action beyond.

CHAPTER 3

Presence

Executive Presence: What it is, and How to "Get" it!

Executive Presence. The holy grail of professional life. A catch-phrase that many executives strive to embody. It is a phrase often mentioned. Leaders we look up to have it and most of the rest of us want it.

But what *is* it?

Merriam Webster defines this type of presence as ". . . the bearing, carriage, or air of a person; *especially*: stately or distinguished bearing."

But does every individual carry an "air"? Does every executive need to be stately? And can a newly minted senior executive always be considered "distinguished"?

In a rather unscientific study, I asked twenty C-level executives from Fortune 1000 companies to describe executive presence. The answers ran the gamut—how one dresses, how one presents themselves, how one shakes a hand, and one's diction.

The important takeaway here: twenty different interview subjects, twenty different answers. There was some overlap, albeit less than I would have expected. It appears that presence, like communication, is intensely personal. It means many different things to many different people. In my opinion, all answers are correct, because executive presence exists in the eye of the beholder.

There are key characteristics and qualities that enhance presence, no matter your precise definition of it. Every executive can go through a basic list, asking questions like the following:

1. **Nonverbal communication.** How do I carry myself when I enter a room? How do I greet someone? How do I introduce myself to someone new? Are there any "comfort gestures" I embrace when uncomfortable? Does my jaw start to move before someone else finishes speaking?

2. **Verbal communication.** How do I deliver a message? Do I purposefully deliver a message, or speak until I invariably lead myself to one? Do I overcompensate with detail? Rely too heavily on acronyms? Understand my audience and focus on delivering information in a way that is easy to process?

3. **Vocal characteristics.** Do I breathe and speak from my diaphragm, or from my chest? Do I utilize tonal changes? Do I inflect? Do I enunciate clearly? Do I pause?

4. **Posture.** Do I "choke" myself when I speak? (Hint, most of us do.) Do I favor one leg or one side? Do I speak toward my audience or toward the floor? Or toward a slide?

5. **Attire.** Do my clothes fit? Am I comfortable in them? Are they appropriate for the situation? What message am I sending with my attire and accessories?

Once individual traits were separated out in the study, there was one word that came up more often than any other: poise—how one handles her- or himself in professional situations. Poise may be the culmination of different ingredients (or characteristics), and it may look different depending on the individual.

Poise and executive presence are both complicated terms. To give you a better idea of what presence encompasses, here are a few more factors:

1. **Listening.** Do I listen or simply wait for an opportunity to speak again? And when listening, am I listening on a superficial level or listening to really identify what is being communicated? So much is communicated in very subtle ways, through word selection, very brief changes in pitch, quick movements, and more.

2. **Listening, part II.** Is it clear to my audience that I am listening? Would every person I speak to describe me as a strong listener? I challenge you to find an executive described as having tremendous "presence" who is not also described as a good listener.

3. **Response, or reaction?** A very wise mentor repeatedly explained to me the difference between responding and reacting. Reacting means an immediate emotional response, while, ideally, responding means careful thought, depersonalizing your response, and understanding that maintaining your composure is as important as anything you might express verbally. Responding is okay. Reacting is not. How do you react? Would your reaction look different fifteen minutes, or fifteen hours later? Full disclosure—this is one of my personal challenges, and I work on it every day.

4. **Approachability.** In my experience, the word that always follows presence is approachable. Are you approachable? Do you make eye contact? Are you easy to talk to? Do you smile? Do you greet every person, regardless of position? I am often

asked what makes someone likable, and the closest I can come to describing it is approachability.

Former U.S. President Bill Clinton, who has less spare time than most, is often described as treating every person as if they are the only one in the room. If someone once responsible for leading the United States can make time to treat everyone with such respect, can't you do the same?

5. **Presentness.** Are you present when you communicate? Is your mind elsewhere? Are you visibly multitasking? Or are you mentally multitasking—something we all do that is just as noticeable?

A client of mine, before he became a wildly successful entrepreneur, approached a famous billionaire at a conference. That billionaire is now, and was at the time, one of the most successful businessmen in the United States. My client, twenty-five years old at the time, had nothing to offer. For those fifteen minutes, my client said that billionaire focused on nothing except for my client. He describes the encounter, twenty years later, as vividly as the day he experienced it. The billionaire was indeed present.

Students I work with at Princeton University describe many of the tech leaders they have had the opportunity to meet through a University program in the same way. Very busy, very successful individuals—and for the time that the students are in front of them, those executives are present. Not aloof.

Which leads to the grand finale: Executive presence isn't necessarily something you *do*; it is an amalgamation of many, many different traits and characteristics, and it has everything to do with the way you communicate. It doesn't exist in a vacuum bag. Like your communication style, it is built over time, not through one meeting or interaction. Every executive has the capacity to have presence.

Body Language: The "7%, 38%, 55% Rule"

One of the key characteristics of executive presence mentioned above is nonverbal communication. Over forty years ago, Dr. Albert Mehrabian, a professor from UCLA, released a study that found 55% of understanding a message is based on body or facial language, 38% is based on tone of voice, and only 7% is based on the words used.

That apparently means that 93% of communication is nonverbal. Ninety-three percent! Very powerful, and cited *ad nauseam* as proof that what you say is much less important than how you say it.

This is all well and good, except for the fact that the statistics are taken out of context . . . Way out of context. Don't just take my word for it.

Professor Mehrabian was studying a very specific communication experience. Here is what he writes about his own study:

> "Total Liking = 7% Verbal Liking + 38% Vocal Liking + 55% Facial Liking.
>
> Please note that this and other equations regarding relative importance of verbal and nonverbal messages were derived from experiments dealing with communications of feelings and attitudes (i.e., like-dislike). Unless a communicator is talking about their feelings or attitudes, these equations are not applicable."

Okay, that was a lot in only two sentences. So what is the message here? Unless it is regarding a specific communication event, with a very specific focus on personal feelings or attitudes, the equation isn't relevant.

While we have no idea just how significant nonverbal communication is according to percentage for other topics, we do know that it still plays a major role in every public presentation.

How you hold your hands, your posture, your eye contact, how you gesture, move, or utilize facial expressions all influence how the audience receives, processes, and interprets your message, whether positively or negatively.

There are countless body language "experts." The majority of advice from these "experts" is fairly rote—hold your hands this way, lack of eye contact means someone is lying, crossing your arms means you are defensive, pointing appears to be rude, and the list goes on and on. Some of this advice may be true. The operative word here is *may*.

Crossing your arms *may* mean you are in a defensive position, pointing *may* appear rude, and looking away *may* mean you are lying. Of course, crossed arms might be a result of cold temperatures, pointing may be inspirational to a certain audience, and a lack of eye contact may be due to shyness or a cultural bias.

The rationale: Every person is an individual, and what works for one person may or may not work for another.

I am an ardent believer that just as no two individuals are alike, no two speaking styles are alike. One body language principle may work for 95% of the population, but it may not work for you!

While different speakers will have different styles, everyone has small body language habits they don't notice, from fidgeting with fingernails to crossing their arms. While they won't cause any problems in day-to-day life (aside from maybe giving away your hand in poker), these habits can be quite distracting when an interviewer is focused on you one-on-one, or an audience is watching you give a presentation. To communicate your message effectively in any context, you want to prevent as many distractions to your audience as possible.

Here are some general rules to follow, potential pitfalls to watch out for, and basic strategies to think about to ensure that you are communicating as effectively as you can from a nonverbal perspective.

POSTURE

Aim for a neutral spine. Posture should be the classic "sit up" or "stand up" straight, as if a string were tied from the top of your head to the ceiling. Do you want to experience what poor posture feels like? Tilt your hips forward, round your shoulders, and walk for five seconds. Then try it with your shoulders back, head straight, spine straight—the difference will be obvious. One trick: pinch your shoulder blades together with a cola can between them—this will open your chest dramatically. From that point, ease into a neutral spine so that your shoulders are squared rather than rounded.

Posture doesn't only matter while you're in front of the audience. Researchers at Harvard University found that engaging in powerful stances *before* presenting, when the audience could not even see the presenter, led to speakers being more confident. "Power posing" increased subjects' feeling of power, and it may have even increased testosterone (which benefits confidence) and decreased the stress hormone cortisol.[10]

GESTURES

"What do you do with your hands?" This is easily one of the most frequent questions I'm asked. My answer: What do you usually do with your hands? Use them!

---

10 Cuddy, Amy J.C., Caroline A. Wilmuth, and Dana R. Carney. "The Benefit of Power Posing Before a High-Stakes Social Evaluation." Harvard Business School Working Paper, No. 13-027, September 2012.

Researchers have found that gesturing matters.[11] Gesturing helps us to remember, both as presenters and as audience members. Gesturing is intuitive. In fact, most of us gesture all day without even realizing it.

In everyday interactions, we use our arms and hands to varying degrees when we talk. I see this every day within my practice. I will record an executive who stands stiff as can be when presenting. I will then record that same executive interacting in conversation with me—but now, the executive is significantly more animated. So how do we merge the two? How can your use of gesturing when presenting be more reflective of your gesturing while in everyday conversation?

When presenting, holding your hands a certain way is not the goal. The goal is to allow your hands and arms to be relaxed when you begin and are most anxious, so that they can move freely as your comfort level increases.

Beginning with your arms at your sides so that your arms and hands are free to move as you warm into your presentation will help you to relax. If that is uncomfortable, a position such as a steeple, that allows you to move your arms and hands freely, will work as well.

As with everything else, it depends on what makes you most comfortable, as long as you avoid distracting your audience! Fast, repeated, or aggressive hand gestures should be kept to a minimum.

FACIAL EXPRESSIONS

I can say with certainty that the nonverbal communication I find to be the most powerful in a presentation setting are

---

11 Cook, Susan Wagner, et al. "Gesturing Makes Memories That Last." *Journal of Memory and Language*, U.S. National Library of Medicine, Nov. 2010, www.ncbi.nlm.nih.gov/pmc/articles/PMC3124384/.

facial expressions. Dr. Paul Ekman, a psychology professor at the University of California, San Francisco, and expert on "micro-expressions" (and inventor of the term) has catalogued over 10,000 expressions we can make with the forty-three facial muscles we have. 10,000!

When it comes to facial expressions, there are two rules to remember. First and foremost, be authentic. Dr. Ekman has proven we are far poorer at faking expressions than we think we are. Do you think that phony smile fooled the audience? Doubt it.

Second, allow people to see your expressions, and be in tune with your content so that your expressions match your intention. Practicing facial expressions doesn't work. Being in the moment with the audience and with your content, regardless of how nervous you are, does work, and will lead you to be more expressive than you think.

Practice will allow you to feel the emotion of what you are talking about so that your expressions match your material. When you are happy, or talking about something that is happy in nature, you will smile.

Focus on making eye contact with all of your audience, and not just with one individual. If you are using notes, or a text, or a PowerPoint slide deck, do not speak while you are looking down or to the side. Speak when you are looking at your audience. When you are looking down, try to remain silent.

"DISTRACTORS" (GROOMING GESTURES)

Grooming gestures—playing with one's hair, fingernails, and jewelry—are common in high-pressure settings. They're caused by nervous energy and a natural desire to appear your best, and often they're not even an issue. Grooming gestures only become a problem when they distract the audience.

These nervous habits, which seem so intrinsic and unavoidable, are, in fact, the easiest to kick—at least for a limited time window such as a presentation.

I tend to roll my watch on my wrist, which is why it isn't on my wrist when I present!

If you have long hair, pull it back or put it up so you don't flick it behind your ear repeatedly. I always tell people to avoid rings, watches, and jewelry on presentation day—if it's not there, you won't play with it. If you don't play with it, there's no chance of distracting your audience, which will keep their attention where it should be: focused on your presentation.

Your Voice Matters!

The next key characteristic is verbal communication. When was the last time you sent an email or a text rather than making a phone call? Chances are, it was within the last twenty-four hours. It is often easier and takes less time and energy. It is also less effective. Our voices matter, and they make an impact on how our message is received. It can impact who gets hired and who doesn't. But again, don't just take my word for it.

Dr. Nick Epley is the John T. Keller Professor of Behavioral Science at the University of Chicago Booth School of Business. He is regularly recognized as a leading behavioral scientist/psychologist (full disclosure—I am a big fan), and his research will not only help you better understand other people, but will improve your understanding of how your own mind works.[12]

While sending written communication is often easier, more convenient, or allows for more personal (or comfortable) expression for the person delivering information, it is not always optimal. Much can get "lost in translation" when there is no voice. Think of the number of times you read something and inferred something from the written message that would have been avoided had you picked up the phone. The human voice is an amazing gift.

Dr. Epley's study, "The Sound of Intellect,"[13] illustrates just how important one's voice is. There is a link to the whole study in the bibliography, but here's a summary of the main findings:

> *A person's mental capacities, such as intellect, cannot be observed directly and so are instead inferred from indirect cues. We predicted that a person's intellect would be conveyed most strongly through a cue closely tied to actual thinking: his or her voice. Hypothetical employers (Experiments 1-3b) and professional recruiters (Experiment 4) watched, listened, or read job candidates' pitches about why they should be hired. Evaluators rated the candidates as more competent, thoughtful, and intelligent when they heard the pitch than when they read it and, as a result, liked the candidate more*

12 Dr. Epley is the author of one of my personal favorite tomes in behavioral science, called *Mindwise: Why We Misunderstand What Others Think, Believe, Feel, and Want*. If you are a student of human interaction (and we all are) or are just interested in learning more about your most valuable possession (your mind), it is a must read.

13 Schroeder, Juliana, and Nicholas Epley. "The Sound of Intellect: Speech Reveals a Thoughtful Mind, Increasing a Job Candidate's Appeal - Juliana Schroeder, Nicholas Epley, 2015." *SAGE Journals*, https://doi.org/10.1177/0956797615572906.

> *and were more interested in hiring the candidate. Adding voice to written pitches, by having trained actors (Experiment 3a) or untrained adults (Experiment 3b) read them, replicated these results. Adding visual cues through video did not influence evaluations beyond the candidate's voice. When conveying one's intellect, it is important for one's voice, quite literally, to be heard.*

There are a lot of gems in this study as it pertains to communication, but if I were to cite just one, it would be summed up in three words: Your voice matters.

I asked Dr. Epley questions about this study a few years ago, and his answers can benefit leaders in every industry:

1. How can CEOs and other organizational leaders most effectively utilize this research?

   > Our data suggests that the medium through which people communicate has a specific effect on how you're viewed by others. If you want your presence of mind to be recognized—the degree to which you've thought hard about a problem, can empathize with someone's circumstance, or have carefully analyzed an issue—then it's essential for your voice, very literally, to be heard. Stripping out your voice and relying on text makes it easier for others to rely on their stereotypes about you when forming impressions. So much of modern communication happens through our fingers. Maintaining voice time is critical.

2. You distinguish between contents and capacity—how would a potential employer define capacity, and what would he or she be "listening" for, based on what you observed?

We refer to mental capacity, and it's simply in our data a judgment about how intelligent, thoughtful, and mentally competent you are. This is a judgment about how well you are able to think, not a judgment about what you happen to be thinking. Our data do not indicate what specific semantic content people are paying attention to. It shows that paralinguistic cues in the voice have an effect on how intellectually capable you are perceived to be. Additional evidence we have suggests that pitch variance is an important cue (intonation in your voice), but other cues such as pauses and volume seem important as well. These cues all suggest you've got a lively mind, and that seems important for these judgments.

3. In your earlier work, you delivered a brilliant analysis about, among many other things, our ability to interpret others. How does your latest study tie in?

   It provides more evidence about the importance of a person's voice for communicating their mind. A person's mind comes through their mouth, more so than the words typed through their fingers.

4. What was your biggest surprise when conducting this study?

   That our professional recruiters, who interview our MBA students for a living, were affected by the presence or absence of a candidate's voice every bit as much as people who imagined being recruiters (but were not selected based on this job). In fact, our professional recruiters actually showed effects that were bigger than our other participants.

Social Psychology, Persuasion, and Public Speaking

Arizona State University professor and best-selling author Dr. Robert Cialdini is widely recognized as the leading authority on the study of influence.

Influencing others isn't achieved through luck or magic—it's about science. Cialdini explains that there are proven ways to help make you more successful as an influencer. He identifies the six key principles of influence as reciprocity, commitment/consistency, social proof, likability, authority, and scarcity. Each of these principles is applicable to the act of presenting and can be utilized to make more effective and impactful presentations.

RECIPROCITY

Reciprocity in public speaking can take many forms, but the most basic is also one of the most effective. When you give the audience a clear understanding of what's in it for them (their interest), they respond with a favorable reaction. One way to achieve this is by answering two questions when preparing your message: What *does* my audience care about? And why should my audience care about *this*?

Another effective way to utilize reciprocity is to give your audience a verbal takeaway that was unexpected—a free tip, a useful piece of information, etc. Especially if you are an expert in your field and your audience has limited access to your expertise, a free and valuable piece of information can go a long way.

COMMITMENT/CONSISTENCY

Getting people to commit during a presentation can be challenging. One way that I have found to be successful is to ask questions based around your audience's interests. But how do you identify those interests?

Through active preparation and research prior to the presentation—this leads to a clearer understanding of what the audience will be looking for from your presentation. Commitment is often gained prior to the presentation even beginning.

SOCIAL PROOF

There is a reason that every toothpaste and gum sold on the market seems to be endorsed by "nine out of ten dentists." This same principle can also work through the effective use of statistics and/or endorsements in a presentation.

Another effective technique is to speak with audience members prior to presenting, and reference them in your presentation. ("When we spoke earlier, Cindy and Deb said . . . ") Just make sure it's nothing too embarrassing!

LIKABILITY

Likability is not something that can be taught. That being said, you can still help sway an audience to be predisposed to like you.

Here are a few suggestions:

- Be authentic (i.e. be yourself).
- Make your presentation about what your audience needs to hear rather than what you want to tell them.
- Be open.
- When appropriate, genuinely smile.

AUTHORITY

Authority when presenting is usually established either a) prior to your presentation or b) through effectively demonstrating your ability to take detailed information and make it accessible to your audience.

Authority is not established by droning on and on about one's credentials or delving so deeply into a subject matter that you are the only one who understands it. Neither is authority achieved through reliance on acronyms, jargon, or the use of sesquipedalia . . .

See, I just did it on purpose!

Sesquipedalian means having many syllables—if your talk is full of words that only you can pronounce or define, you will fail to influence anyone.

SCARCITY

When it comes to communication, I equate scarcity with brevity. Entice your audience and leave them wanting more!

After most presentations, the audience is worn out. Stand outside any conference venue and you will constantly hear, "I couldn't wait for that to end." Very rarely do you hear, "That was riveting—I could have listened for hours." Aim for the latter.

A second way to utilize scarcity is to offer enticing information—just enough to get your audience interested—and then . . . pause. Pause for a longer amount of time than expected. This will create a "scarcity effect" for a crucial moment in a presentation. An advanced scarcity technique is to allow that tantalizing information to serve as a feeder for the question-and-answer period.

Though the material covered in a single book chapter can never completely describe what executive presence is or how to "get" it, this should get you started. How you communicate non-verbally can greatly impact how your message is received, from posture to gestures and everything in between. Your voice matters, so consider picking up the phone (for a call, not a text!) instead of typing out your next email. And finally, your actions and patterns of behavior influence those around you. The ability to be both self- and socially aware will take you far, so go forth with poise and presence!

CHAPTER 4

Preparation

I am often asked, "What is the secret to successful public speaking?" My answer is usually not what people want to hear. The "secret" is hard work, preparation, and practice! Would anyone in the world expect Lionel Messi to not play soccer for a year, come on the field and be the greatest football player in the world a year later? Of course not. Somehow, this is what many speakers desire—give a presentation, be unhappy with the results, and then do nothing until the next opportunity. Practice and preparation are the most valuable keys.

Prepare Like an NBA All-Star

Eight hundred "makes."

A trainer hired to help Team USA prepare for the Olympics recalled his experience working with Laker legend Kobe Bryant. Bryant woke up his trainer to begin practicing at 4 a.m., and didn't conclude until seven hours later, after conditioning, weight work, and making 800 shots. *He had to be done at 11 a.m. because he had a scrimmage with other Olympic (NBA) All-Stars!*

So, what does an NBA legend have to do with public speaking? Bryant is one of the greatest athletes of our lifetime, and he *always* made sure to practice *with intention*.[14]

Practice and preparation are simple in concept, but not as easy to actually do. However, they are integral to the success of any presentation. They are also the biggest factors in helping ease anxiety and nerves prior to a presentation.

I present a few times every week, and I practice a presentation a minimum of seven times (usually more) before I actually present. Every single time.

I begin the preparation phase knowing that the presentation will go through numerous iterations prior to being delivered. That is the beauty of the process—seeing what works and what doesn't. During the preparation phase, I focus on:

- Determining what my core message is
- How to support that message
- How to open with impact
- How to transition between supports
- How to include my audience
- How to close with power and move my audience to act

Practice Like a Professional

Let's move to the next phase, which is the beginning of practicing. I work with an outline for the initial practice session to

14 Astramskas, David. "Storytime: Team USA trainer tells a story about Kobe's insane work ethic."*Ballislife.com,* 6 Mar. 2014, https://ballislife.com/storytime-team-usa-trainer-kobe/.

determine how I might want to transition, how to interact with the audience, what works, and what doesn't. There are a number of ways every person reading this can practice like a professional. Here are six tips:

1. **Determine your message** (as well as your key supporting points). Determine what your message is and why your audience should care. Write out your whole speech, and then pare it down to bullet points. From there, shorten your points even more to leave only key words and phrases. This process not only helps to sharpen the presentation, it also helps to internalize it—after all, every rewrite is a form of practice. This has to happen prior to practicing, although practicing will help shape this as well.

2. **Power of video.** Today, everyone has a smartphone. Set it on the counter and tape yourself. While this is not particularly enjoyable, it is revealing, and will help you to determine what is and isn't working.

3. **Find a friend.** Practice in front of audiences who may or may not know anything about the subject matter. This a) ramps up the pressure a bit and b) provides great feedback as to the power of the message and the delivery of that message.

4. **Back to the camera.** Refinement time. At this point, the presentation, or your portion of it, has really begun to take shape. This is where your 800 "makes" come into play. Tape yourself again—look at your movement, get a feel for your cadence, and lend a sharper ear to your vocal qualities (pitch, rate, inflection, tone, projection, etc.).

5. **Advanced "mime work."** To work on nonverbal delivery, and to really "feel" what I am expressing, I will actually

practice, on tape, delivering the presentation without words. My mouth won't open. My puppy gets very confused, and I might look a bit odd, but the results are telling, as I am able to focus not only on posture and gesturing, but on facial movements and expressions as well.

6. **Stop.** My goal with preparation and practice is not to be scripted, but to be so comfortable with my message and myself that I can be totally present when the time comes. On presentation day, I will only practice my open, as at this point the message is already "in my DNA." I will focus on relaxing and working through strategies to help deal with any anxiety I might be facing.

I believe that with practice and preparation, every person can be a successful presenter. *Every* person. But this is only true if you put the time in. Ask yourself how many legends, in any field, succeed without practice. Then start preparing for your next meeting or presentation!

Demosthenes and Modern Oratory

Demosthenes is one of my favorite orators to study. Unfortunately, I never had the opportunity to see or hear him in person, as he passed away in 323 BCE. He was a prominent Greek statesman and legendary orator of ancient Athens, and some of his most famous (and my favorite) addresses were related to his opposition to King Philip II of Macedon. Demosthenes is another relevant example of dedication to practice and preparation.

Demosthenes actually grew up with a speech impediment. However, it didn't stop him from achieving his dream of becoming a great orator. As a child, he was ridiculed early and often for his deficiencies, but he never quit. Here are a few things he was rumored to have done to overcome his speech impediment and attain his goal:

- He self-corrected his defective elocution by practicing speaking with pebbles in his mouth.
- He prepared himself to overcome the distraction of noise by speaking in stormy weather on the seashore.
- He recited verses while running to improve his breathing and cadence.
- He sometimes passed two or three months in an underground cave practicing his oratory.
- While cave dwelling, he would shave half of his head to prevent himself from leaving as a commitment to practicing.

While I would never encourage you to live in a cave or shave half your head, there are more realistic steps you can take to practice and improve your speaking in the "Practice Like a Professional" section above.

And Demosthenes isn't the only great orator who began life with a disadvantage.

Woodrow Wilson is not often one of the first figures that come to mind when remembering legendary orators of the past, but he should be. The dedication and attention he gave to developing his communication skills from an early age may not make it into many public-speaking books, but they should.

The challenges that the young Woodrow Wilson had to face as a communicator were significant. He was not a "natural." He was dyslexic, had attention issues, and did not exude confidence. But he studied the great orators. He practiced and practiced and practiced. He took advantage of every opportunity. His determination and self-education paid off.

Wilson made becoming a powerful, persuasive, effective communicator one of his top priorities as a student at Princeton University and as a young professor. This skillset served Wilson well as he went on to become President of Princeton University, Governor of New Jersey, and ultimately the President of the United States.

President Wilson has left us with many powerful orations. In a 1912 campaign address (I believe the only audio clip that exists of Wilson speaking), his diction, inflection, volume, and rate are notable.

These elements of speech are worth considering, as they affect what your audience determines is important or impactful. For instance, take a sentence like, "Please, take the garbage out now." On paper, that sentence can be taken any number of ways, and we're not sure which one is intended. However, if I stress "Please," it can change the entire meaning either to something semi-endearing or respectful to something downright frustrating or hostile. The same goes with "now" or any of the other words. A good way to practice these elements is to take a generic sentence from any source—newspaper, magazine, television commercial—and practice changing the meaning of what you're saying without changing any of the words (so using only your inflection, rate, intonation, etc). So we're all on the same page, here are definitions for some of the less intuitive elements:

- **Diction:** Speaking style or choice of words or phrasing
- **Intonation:** The pattern or melody of pitch changes when speaking
- **Inflection:** Modulation of the voice or pitch

President Wilson's contributions to Princeton, New Jersey, and the United States are many. So are his contributions to oratory and public speaking—but none are more important than the necessity of practice and preparation!

Steve Jobs: Preparation, Practice, and Public Speaking

Over the past decade, very few (if any) executives have had the impact on how we communicate that Steve Jobs did. For news to last through multiple cycles is quite rare; however, the passing of Jobs did just that—and for good reason.

What made Steve Jobs so popular was not just innovation or new technology. He was also an extremely effective communicator. His public-speaking skills had everything to do with fundamentals, starting with the crucial (yet often ignored) step of extensive preparation. The preparation and practice that went into each product launch or public presentation was evident. Each presentation became an event in and of itself.

Here are two of my favorite Steve Jobs presentations and their key takeaways.

THE ORIGINAL IPHONE LAUNCH

Steve Jobs launched the first iPhone on January 9, 2007, and ever since, the world of mobile phones has never been the same. Here are some of my favorite aspects of this memorable presentation:

- Very limited use of slides (no "Death by PowerPoint")
- Limited content on each slide
- Effective use of movement
- Use of the "Power Pause"
- Effective gesturing
- Simple, conversational language. I am convinced that one of the reasons Apple is the market leader is not only because of the ease-of-use of the product line, but also the ease-of-explanation as to how the products work and what they offer.

STANFORD COMMENCEMENT (2005)

This is one of the most moving speeches I have heard and seen in the past decade, and it affects me every time I watch it.

- The use of story (amazing storytelling)
- The use of repetition
- Use of summation (every story is neatly summarized with a memorable takeaway)

Look at these unforgettable words:

"Almost everything—all external expectations, all pride, all fear of embarrassment or failure—these things just fall away in the face of death, leaving only what is truly important. Remembering that you are going to die is the best way I know to avoid the trap of thinking you have something to lose. You are already naked. There is no reason not to follow your heart."

~ Steve Jobs

"Focus" Your Presentation

Focus groups have long been the domain of political campaigns. They can be used to test messages, appearances, images, sound bites, oppositional research, and more. Focus groups have become a staple in the corporate world, where products, messages, slogans, ad campaigns, and competition are regularly tested.

Litigators effectively utilize focus groups to test key messages. So do candidates for office. The true value of a focus group is not necessarily to discover why a candidate or product is well liked, but rather, why it isn't liked. This information can be used to improve a product or change minds.

I am a believer that every person, whether a front-line associate or CEO, can benefit from running a mini focus group prior to a high-stakes speech, investor pitch, or presentation. Again, this is not to validate how "good" your presentation is, but to see where there are soft spots, weaknesses, and areas for improvement. Here are a few steps to set up a quick, effective focus group before your next big speech:

1. **Know your audience.** Who will be represented in the audience? Employees? Board members? Investors? Have a representative in your focus group from each of the various sectors that will be in the audience. The group does not have to be big, nor does it have to be formal—it just has to be representative.

2. **Friends are not always your friends.** When running focus groups, shy away from having friends participate as a focus group member. What you are looking for is distance from the issue. People whom you know, respect, and trust, but do not necessarily spend all of your time with, often offer the best feedback.

3. **Friends are not always your friends, part II.** For similar reasons, avoid having people participate who are very close to each other. It tends to skew the dynamic and often overpowers the group, leading to missing key feedback.

4. **Preparation.** I like to throw just about everything that I am planning on speaking about out there. Sometimes I am too close to the topic and miss things that might be more effective or beneficial to my audience. An unprepared speech or presentation will focus all of the attention on delivery and not much on the message, meaning that you will get half of the value. Spend some time preparing.

5. **Ask!** If you are a front-line associate, ask your mentor to sit in to represent executives. Conversely, C-level executives often balk at having a lower-level associate watch a presentation first. There is undoubtedly some risk, but I have done it a number of times and it has worked every time. The key is to identify the right person to participate. You are looking for a very small group. Again, not to validate how "good" you are, but to offer new opinions and bring a different perspective.

Your focus group can be as formal or informal as you want or are able to make it—the key is to get a variety of opinions on your presentation (preferably from a group that's representative of your future audience).

Whether you choose to hold a focus group or use one (or several!) of the other methods discussed to prepare for a presentation, the most important thing is simply that you follow through with it. Great orators and influencers have all shown us how important practice is and how far it can take you. Rehearse your presentation, find a friend, video yourself—whatever works best for you.

Okay, so you are now through the first section of this book. Yikes. There is a lot to this public speaking stuff, isn't there? That's why it is so important to experiment with different techniques and see what works best for *you*. Every person is unique, and that carries forward to a person's communication style. Think of them as special tools in your "toolbox."

So rather than repeat techniques, let's remember what we know:

You know that fear is normal—helpful, even—and you aren't alone in that fear. Those worrisome physiological quirks (sweating, shaking, narrowing vision) are merely your body responding to stress and preparing you for action, but you can make that work for you through tactics such as those you have just read about.

We know that to create and deliver an engaging presentation, it all starts with your message. What does the audience need to know, and why should they care? Once the message is defined, it has to be backed up with supporting evidence, or the audience won't invest. If they begin to drift anyway, remember there are some "life preservers" among the sea of techniques above.

We all have a "presence," whether we want to or not. Nonverbal communication is extremely important, and we aren't always aware of the messages we send. Through utilizing some of the techniques outlined above, you will be able to offer yourself to your audience authentically and genuinely without having to focus on the thoughts running through your mind, like Will Ferrell in *Talladega Nights*—"Where do I hold my hands?"

Once you're aware of fear and anxiety's role, you have a well-developed message and presentation structure, and you know how to present yourself in front of your audience, the last step, and some might argue the most crucial step, is to practice. Without practice, most of the techniques above are just that—techniques on a piece of paper. Practice is what makes them uniquely yours.

No one expects athletes to perform well without practicing, and you shouldn't expect that of yourself either. Record yourself, present for a friend, or even develop a focus group to get more feedback on your presentation before it's go time.

The tips in Part 1, when worked with and practiced, will help you develop a core set of skills for making and delivering presentations. Read on to Part 2 for strategies to implement those skills in a variety of situations.

PART 2

Strategies

CHAPTER 5

Business

I know what many of you might be saying: "Ok, Eventoff, this is all well and good, but I only give one or two big presentations a year, if that. The vast majority of my time communicating professionally is spent in meetings, on conference calls, at seminars, and at horrific networking events. How does any of this information apply to any of these situations?" These are great and fair questions.

First and foremost, all of the strategies and tactics you have read so far are directly applicable to these smaller situations outside of formal presentations. The messaging section, for instance, is critical for every communication opportunity and will improve the length and effectiveness of every business interaction. Adding calls-to-action in key meetings and conference calls can eliminate the need for a follow-up conference call to discuss what the next steps might be (We've all sat through meetings and left thinking, "What was the point of that?" only to return to your office seeing a calendar invite for yet another meeting on the same subject). Opening more engagingly, structuring more effectively, closing with impact, and having clear messaging and takeaways are invaluable in every corporate communication situation. And in the famous words of so many people . . . that's not all!

In this chapter, we will dig deeper into strategies and tactics for communicating more effectively in corporate settings.

Seven Tips to Crush Your Next Conference Call

We have almost all been victims, and many of us offenders, of "twenty seconds of silence"—those twenty seconds after someone asks a question on a call and mentions your name. Those twenty seconds you fight to find the mute button you pressed while ignoring the call content and working on emails, document prep, and sometimes taking other calls. Those twenty seconds before everyone on the call hears ". . . uh, uh, I'm here. It's Matt here . . ."

When I ask executives to tell me what they consider to be public speaking, I have heard almost everything imaginable, from speeches and presentations to rallying cries at a child's little league game.

However, one event I never hear about without prompting is actually one of the most common forms of public communication. It occurs on a regular basis for almost every individual in the corporate world, and it is also the most fraught with peril. The scourge of the modern executive. The captor of thousands (or maybe millions) of hours each and every day. The dreaded . . . conference call!

Conference calls have become so routine and so standard that they are often not considered what they really are: an opportunity to stand out and present with superiors on the line, an opportunity to drive a message forward, and an opportunity to influence through communication. Unfortunately, these are often lost opportunities.

Here are a few ways to make sure these opportunities don't slip through your fingers:

1. **Get a headset.** A telephone cradled between your ear and your shoulder is distracting. Having someone on speaker allows too much ambient noise. A headset allows freedom. It also allows you to . . .

2. **Perform the call standing.** Yes, that's right, standing. Movement is an essential component of public communication, enhancing your delivery as well as helping you keep focus as if there were a live audience in front of you.

3. **Turn off technology.** Conference calls don't just allow for multitasking—they invite it. You wouldn't text or email while delivering a speech or presentation to a board, or even a team. Having your computer on, or even your phone, is an invitation for distraction.

4. **Pay attention to your voice (tone, pitch, etc.).** It is all you have. Without nonverbal cues, your audience will be relegated to verbal ones. That means your voice has outsized impact. Keep that in mind when delivering information. Context is built around your verbal cues.

5. **Avoid the urge.** Not having an audience in front of you can also allow for a cluttered desk and scattered notes. Prepare as if you were walking into a presentation . . . because you are! Having key messages and supporting bullet points can be helpful. Having too much information can distract you, which will distract your audience.

6. **Close the blinds.** If at all possible, try to choose your location so that you can cut out as many distractions as possible. It's hard to focus with people looking into your office.

7. **Prepare.** Determine your key messages. Why does your information matter to each participant? How can they use that

information? Be in a position to listen. Be active. Be involved. Take advantage of the situation.

And finally, be careful with the mute button. The twenty seconds it takes you to hit it again can send a clear message that you aren't present. It also invites every other participant to treat you the same way.

Effective Meetings

Meetings! We all attend them, participate in them, and to varying degrees, loathe them. I'm sure you can agree that the majority of meetings are not exceedingly organized or efficient. They are also often very time consuming, and they can be expensive.

> "If you had to identify, in one word, the reason why the human race has not achieved and never will achieve its full potential, that word would be 'meetings.'"
>
> **Dave Barry**

Numerous studies have estimated that over ten million meetings occur each day.[15] A University of Arizona/ University of Tulsa study estimates meeting expenses range from $30 million to over $100 million a year—and that's from a decade ago![16]

Meetings can be an organization's silent killer—both

15 "America Meets a Lot. An Analysis of Meeting Length, Frequency and Cost." *Attentiv,* 23 Sept. 2015, attentiv.com/america-meets-a-lot/.

16 Romano, N.C., and J.F. Nunamaker. "Meeting Analysis: Findings from Research and Practice." *Proceedings of the 34th Annual Hawaii International Conference on System Sciences*, 2001, https://doi.org/10.1109/hicss.2001.926253.

losing the company money and ruining morale. If an organization had a project that was continually draining the company of money, leading nowhere, and causing top employees to leave, what do you think it might do? Perhaps get rid of it, or at least cut the scope of it down.

I have worked with countless senior executives who have meetings practically all day long, every day. No time to work on projects. No time to return phone calls. And barely enough time to use the facilities between meetings! When asked about when they actually find the time to do the work, the answer is always the same: at night.

When employees are in meetings all day, an organization doesn't just lose productivity, employee satisfaction, and a boatload of money—it also loses groundbreaking ideas, new concepts, and new approaches. That's because meetings can be draining and take up valuable work time.

But as we all know, we can't just cut meetings out entirely. However, we can make them a lot more efficient and hold less of them. It's like the saying, "Work smarter, not harder." Well, "Meet smarter, not more often."

Here are a few steps you can take during meetings to save your company time and money.

1. **Set an agenda.** Set a well-defined agenda and detail what's going to be discussed.

2. **Clear call-to-action.** What is the purpose of the meeting, and what should be accomplished? What does success look like? A document? A decision? An agreement? Even if you don't achieve every meeting objective, have clear objectives laid out in writing, and discuss where you are with each before the meeting ends.

3. **Distinct expectations for every employee.** Who is responsible for what (both before the meeting begins and when it wraps up)? Who is responsible for following up on issues or calls-to-action? Make sure you articulate responsibilities out loud. Don't just assume someone knows it is his or her responsibility.

4. **Hard start, but aim to end early.** Always start on time, and end as soon as the agenda is complete. Giving time back is a gift, and ending over harms your meeting outcome (since everyone will dwell on it) and everyone's next task. Over time, this will show others that your meetings are efficient and effective, and they should come ready to get down to business.

5. **Break the cycle.** Have one or two fewer formal meetings a week and see what happens. Give defined assignments and allow people a bit more time to accomplish them, rather than them scurrying to create a last-minute work product in their "free time."

6. **Film a few meetings.** It sounds tedious, and you certainly don't want to film every meeting, but if you lead over twenty-five meetings a year, the one-hour investment of watching the tape will show you where meetings go off track and where you lose time. One taped meeting can do wonders for helping you identify ways to "meet smarter."

7. **Communication training.** If you were paying each employee by the hour (and not by salary), meetings would be a lot more concise—or else! It is critical that every member of your team knows how to put together a message and deliver that message accurately, concisely, and clearly.

Time is a precious commodity. It is crucial that employees can convey and articulate concepts, arguments, and facts succinctly and quickly. Senior executives simply don't have time for an employee to take twenty minutes to explain a point that could have been made in two.

Influencing During a Meeting

Everyone is around the conference table. Open computers, some folks texting, a deck loaded up on the screen, a white board ready to meet marker. This is a big one. Budgets will be determined. So will future workflow . . . So how do you prepare? This checklist of questions needing your answers is a great place to start (and continue as the meeting evolves):

1. Determine who is who in the audience. Who is the decision-maker? Who influences the decision-maker?
2. What is important to the audience?
3. Develop relationships before making requests. For example, think "How can I help them?" instead of only "Please do this."
4. Ask before you need to. Test your ideas out before you launch them with your audience through a Q&A.
5. Utilize past results and partnerships with that person/team.
6. Frame issues as potential opportunities rather than problems. If you identify an issue/opportunity, think about what the solution could be. That way you're bringing up an opportunity /problem and also a solution/idea.
7. Have a second (and third) idea or solution.
8. Empathy. Show that you can see yourself walking in the other person's shoes.

Buzzwords Must Die

Happy Monday!

Welcome to your first day at ABC Corporation. We are honored and humbled by your decision to join our team.

Before diving into the weeds, let's level set and take a look at ABC Corp from 30,000 feet. At ABC Corporation, we believe there is no "I" in team. We believe we are part of a paradigm shift, and our aim every day is to move the needle.

Before we circle back, let's put a pin in this topic and move forward. #ABCCorpRules

As part of your onboarding, you will learn everything you need to know to proactively be a value-add. Okay? So, at the end of the day, here's what it means. We will stay out of silos. We won't boil the ocean, looking instead for blue ocean strategies. Now, before I disappear and go out of pocket, let's talk about another topic today . . .

BUZZWORDS!

If you have attended a meeting, ever, you have encountered "buzzwords" or "buzz-phrases." It's that simple. I would venture to guess that if you have attended a meeting, ever, you have probably used them. I certainly fall into that category. Many of us have go-to phrases that we may not even realize we regularly use.

Are buzzwords effective? Do audiences enjoy hearing them?

In another very unscientific poll, done both in person and on social media, this topic evoked a visceral reaction from almost every person. There was no shortage of "most annoying buzzwords."

Aside from being annoying, what is the damage from using buzzwords or buzz-phrases? What harm can the use of these phrases do?

It is likely that a few members of your audience don't understand them. We are living in a time where messaging comes at each of us at a speed that makes it impossible to digest, which means important information may be lost when a message is filled with jargon, acronyms, and buzzwords, especially if your audience doesn't understand them.

Let's say that an audience, whether a small meeting or a full auditorium, actually does understand your references. If an audience is focused on a buzzword or phrase, it becomes harder to focus on the message. That doesn't help the effective delivery of that message.

So what can replace buzzwords? The answers and best alternatives are stories, examples, and commonly understood analogies.

While buzzwords don't necessarily help audience members relate to or understand information, examples, stories, and analogies usually do. And helping audiences relate to the information being presented is a key responsibility of the presenter!

Standard language is also key. Most of the most memorable orations and presentations in history contain standard language (for the period they took place) and have stood the test of time. President Lincoln's Gettysburg Address contains 272 words, of which at least 200 consist of a single syllable. No buzzwords.

For instance, most people don't say, "I am going to retire for a number of hours to recharge my internal and external facilities to better engage with the day tomorrow." Most people say, "I am going to bed." Standard language allows an audience to focus on a message rather than try to understand what a word or phrase means.

Explore using alternatives to buzzwords. It will make for more effective and impactful communication.

Creating a Conversation

A speech is not a solo act, rather, think of a speech as a conversation. While only one party may be speaking, all parties are communicating. Looking away, shaking one's head, raising one's brow, showing lack of interest or a face anchored in stoicism are all forms of communication—and are all part of a conversation. Smiling, nodding, clapping, cheering, and riveted attentiveness are also part of a conversation. Walking out of a conference room and doing nothing is part of the conversation too, though usually the end of it.

So what can you do to ensure that a speech or presentation is in fact a productive conversation? Here are just a few ways:

- **Involve your audience.** Do not talk *at* the audience; speak *with* them.
- **Pay attention to personal pronouns.** I tend to shy away from using a lot of "I" and "me" and instead focus more on "we" and "us" as much as possible.
- **Really involve your audience.** When I am presenting on communication or rhetoric, I occasionally involve an audience early on by asking a question addressed to one or two participants right away. I also sometimes do it in the middle of the speech. Not a confrontational question. Not a heavy

question. I very rarely ask a controversial question but instead focus on a question to generate a very short response.

Here is an example: If I am giving a presentation on the need for expediency in speech, I might pick someone out and ask, "How would you feel if I told you this presentation was going to last fifty minutes? How about five minutes?" Or "At what point in a presentation do you start tuning the presenter out?"

Though it appears to be spontaneous, it is anything but. In fact, it is a calculated move to engage the audience, raise attentiveness, and take the conversation to the next level.

Networking for those who HATE Networking

Networking can feel forced and artificial for both introverts and extroverts, because, well, it often is. Networking shouldn't be a numbers game; it should be focused on quality over quantity. This might mean not doing large, organized events, but focusing instead on smaller events or simply one-on-one interactions.

I've found that a highly effective technique for networking, especially for those who tend to dislike it, is the buddy system. It is often much easier to introduce someone else to someone you know, rather than introducing yourself to a stranger. Attending events with a friend or colleague and utilizing the time to introduce each other to individuals that only one person knows can ease some anxiety and allow for more comfortable transitions to conversations. It is also much easier to talk about someone else's great attributes (something that makes most of us uncomfortable when asked to do it about ourselves).[17]

I believe the biggest secret to effective networking is a skill that most individuals naturally possess. That secret is this: *listen*. Simply listen. Say hi, introduce yourself by first name, and then just listen. Most people will talk to fill the silence. People generally like to talk about themselves, about their businesses, their interests, and areas where they are looking to grow. Typically, the more you listen, the more favorable the impression you leave, which is a key to developing a future relationship.

Small Talk is a Big Deal

FACTS ABOUT SMALL TALK

1. No one is really comfortable engaging in small talk with new acquaintances (yeah . . . it's a bit awkward).
2. Pre-programmed questions and statements come across as, well, pre-programmed.
3. The art of small talk is that it's NEVER about you—it's about the other person.
4. There are no rules, just guides. Setting rules makes small talk stay small.
5. Small talk is like public speaking. It's intimidating, and it takes practice.

17 Having someone talk you up helps establish authority, as Caldini would put it, or ethos, as Aristotle would. This helps you become more sought after while networking, or more persuasive while speaking (your introduction to your speech matters). The science behind this shows this effect is still realized even if the person talking you up is connected to you.

6. People like to talk about themselves.
7. Remember fact #6.

So . . . I'm uncomfortable. What do I do?

- Relax
- Smile
- Make eye contact
- Say "hi"
- Introduce yourself

REMEMBER THE FOLLOWING

- Observe and ask questions about what you see.
- When you are approached, remember the Golden Rule: treat others as you would like to be treated.
- Don't use one-word answers.
- If you know the people you are talking to and the person approaching doesn't, introduce them.
- Keep it comfortable. Avoid topics such as politics, religion, family, relationships, etc.
- Know when to leave or exit.

"It was great talking to you, but now I need to ..."

"I'll see you at _____ in _____ ..."

"I have to get to a _____, thank you again ..."

THE "DON'T" LIST

- **Don't think that no one is looking when you attend a networking event.** In fact, someone is always looking! Picking food off a buffet with your fingers, leaving a dirty plate next to a serving tray, spitting food on the floor, picking your nose (yes, I've seen it happen more than once), etc.
- **Don't have "Paparazzi Eyes."** Nothing is more insulting than someone gazing past you, as you are talking to them, to see if someone "more important" is on the way into the room.
- **Don't look at your phone or text while someone is speaking to you.** Also, having a conversation while the presenter is speaking is not fair to the presenter and is disturbing to other participants.
- **Don't assume that the biggest name in the room is the one that will be most important to you.**
- **Don't waste the opportunity.** If a person is interesting, don't be shy—tell them so! Tell them what you enjoyed or found interesting and strike up a conversation.

Business is hard enough as it is. Just a few of the obstacles standing between you and your work include deadlines, meetings, conference calls, the dreaded after-work networking event, the obligatory holiday party . . . With the strategies outlined here, events that were once objects of dread will not only become more palatable, but with some work and, as always, practice, they will even become strengths that help you grow and stand out.

! 1
@ 2
# 3
$ 4
Q
W
E
A
tab
caps lock
shift
fn

CHAPTER 6

Technology

Treat technology like it should be treated: as a helpful tool, not as a replacement for the presenter. From PowerPoint to smartphones, it is important to realize how and when to effectively use technology to your advantage when giving a presentation. And it isn't just useful on stage—from email to social media to Zoom, we utilize technology constantly in our professional relationships. The more we understand the ins and outs of the technology we use every day, the better we will be at presenting ourselves through our technology.

PowerPoint Rules

PowerPoint (PPT) has taken over the corporate universe. Since its launch by Microsoft in 1990, PowerPoint (along with other presentation programs since then) has become a staple in meeting and conference rooms throughout the world. A *BusinessWeek* article estimated that 350 PowerPoint presentations *are given each second* around the globe—350 every second![18]

When it comes to PowerPoint, there are many, many "rules" on number of slides per deck, words per slide, letters per word,

18 "Death to PowerPoint!" *Bloomberg.com*, Bloomberg, 30 Aug. 2012, www.bloomberg.com/news/articles/2012-08-30/death-to-powerpoint.

and more. Most are well intentioned, and some offer interesting and useful ideas. However, I do not believe they are all universally applicable.

I err toward brevity, whether it's with words per slide, number of slides, or elsewhere. While not hard and fast rules, here are a number of suggestions that can help you utilize PowerPoint effectively and efficiently:

1. **PowerPoint is not a presentation.** PowerPoint is a **tool** to **accentuate** or **enhance** a presentation. It is a slide deck—that's all. It isn't a presentation.

2. **Create an outline of your presentation before you place it into PowerPoint** (or Google Slides, or Prezi, or whatever other presentation software you utilize). All too often, an executive sees a presentation "pop up" on his or her schedule, pulls up the blank PowerPoint deck, and starts plugging information into it. Resist the urge! Go through the planning process as if you were presenting without a deck. *Then* go back and accentuate your presentation with facts, figures, graphics, etc.

3. **Know your audience.** Some audiences require more detailed slides than others. Either way, you can rest assured that anyone reading the slide as you present is not focused on you or what you are saying. It isn't possible.

4. **Reduce the detail.** Even if you feel your audience does require more detail, remember, your audience is only human! Do not overwhelm them with detail upon detail upon detail in each and every slide.

   Slides should accentuate and enhance a presentation—not replace it. That being said, many organizations expect "pre-reads" with detailed information. If that is the case, or if your organization expects detail-laden slides, try placing the detail or pre-reads in the appendix, rather than having it on the screen during the actual presentation.

Including more information at the end affords you the ability to reference or advance to the detailed slide if you are asked, but not bore or exhaust your audience if you are not.

5. **Use graphics.** Graphics, short video clips, and illustrations can be very, very powerful. Illustrations can reinvigorate a tired audience. The key is to make them relevant, short, and powerful.

6. . . . **But don't use space-fillers.** Use images to illustrate, not to fill space. Superfluous graphics and illustrations that do not relate to your subject matter, or add to the point you are making, only draw attention away from your message. Prepackaged designs are often disruptive or distracting.

7. **Ideas, bullet points, and keywords.** Many people like to utilize slides to keep focused, almost as virtual notes. That can work effectively. Keywords or bullet points that trigger a speaker can be very helpful and beneficial. I never have more than one idea on a slide, and I try to limit bullet points to three and words per bullet point to four.

8. **Don't talk to the slide.** If you are following along, do not speak as you look at the slide. Look at the slide, absorb the information, turn to the audience, and then speak. You do not want to project your attention, or your voice, toward the screen.

9. **Font size is important.** If your audience is straining to see, they are not focusing on your message or what you are saying. "Can you see now? How about now?"

10. **Limit the number of slides.** Just because everyone else uses fifty slides does not mean you have to! Just because every other person has a slide for every last detail doesn't mean you should. Accentuate your presentation; don't replace yourself with slides as the presenter.

Your PowerPoint Deck: Five Ways to Get it Right

You've spent countless hours preparing and thousands in travel expenses, and yet it all comes down to this one moment: the pitch! Your team has worked on it in meetings, during conference calls, and over emails, reviewing, constructing, deconstructing, and tweaking the PowerPoint presentation that will determine your success . . . or will it?

Maybe you are the one being pitched. You might have presentation commitments of your own, including justifying the expense of your department before the CFO. Or perhaps you are presenting the agency of choice to your CEO.

I can think of countless presentations that have either helped win or helped lose the pitch. However, PowerPoint slides are only part of a presentation. If slides were enough, there would be no reason for a presentation. You could just email the deck to the client and that would be it. Since it isn't, you would think that most agencies and in-house practitioners spend as much time practicing the delivery of the presentation as they do preparing the slides, right?

Not quite. We all know what usually happens. Endless hours are spent putting the deck together, making changes to it up until an hour before the pitch—sometimes even right before. Then there is travel to the presentation site, overcoming jet lag, getting the team together to regroup . . . and maybe getting a chance to practice a few minutes before entering the boardroom. You might have scheduled a conference call before the presentation to discuss roles, who will address what, and who is responsible for different lines of questioning. In the end, the balance between preparing the deck and practicing the presentation is skewed dramatically.

A well-delivered presentation with only a few or even no slides will *always* succeed over a poorly delivered presentation with superior slides. Again, if slides were enough, you would not need to present!

When it comes to a presentation, you have to ask yourself the following questions: How does the team gel? How do individual team members answer questions? How are transitions handled? Who do team members look to when they are unsure? Who is uncomfortable presenting? What personality traits may turn off an audience member? How succinct is each team member? Who reviewed this only a few minutes before coming in and is woefully unprepared? Who disengages when others speak?

These are all questions that will never be answered by a slide deck. These questions and countless others like them are the reason you are presenting in person rather than just emailing your presentation to the client.

Delivery matters as much as content, and preparation should reflect that.

So how do you prepare when time is limited, the client demands a thorough deck, and team members are spread all over the place? Here are a few suggestions:

1. **Narrate as you create.** When preparing slides (even the first iteration), determine who will be delivering them. That person MUST have input into the creation of the slide. Watching

someone deliver information of which he or she has no ownership is painful and obvious.

2. **Live is better.** Try to get together to practice for a few hours in the weeks, days, and evenings prior to the presentation. You will see things in person that need tweaking that you would never notice over a live conference call or video, like movement of team members or transitions between presenters. These small adjustments can have a huge impact.

3. **If live isn't an option, then utilize technology.** Video presence, while not optimal, still allows you to practice individual parts of your presentation "live." You can also record the call and watch it later to help critique each other.

4. **The evening before.** Every team member needs to be in sync before a critical presentation. It's a good idea to get everyone together the night before to review and get comfortable with the presentation. If even one team member arrives late to the meeting or forgets something important, it can cause the entire group to fall out of sync.

5. **Practice saves time.** You will have extraneous information in your deck that you won't realize if you don't practice. Unfortunately, your audience will. Practice your presentation and trim out the superfluous information. It'll end up saving you time when it matters most.

When Technology Comes to Work: Eleven Tips

While this is not a definitive guide by any means, these eleven tips will help you safely navigate the new workplace and avoid undesirable situations when it comes to the interface of work and technology:

1. **Smartphones are not always associated with work.** Justly or unjustly, tablets and smartphones are often associated with activities such as texting, games, and other non-work activities (unlike laptops). Be aware of these associations when you pull out your phone during a meeting.
2. **Tell us!** Many people (including myself) like to take notes digitally. If you do pull out a smartphone or tablet during a meeting to take notes, make sure to tell other attendees, "I use my iPad to take notes." This will prevent others from wondering if you are scrolling TikTok or checking Facebook.
3. **Social media.** These days, many companies have a social media policy—and every organization should! If you have work friends who use social media, they may realize you were actually using your device to tweet or post something to Instagram during a meeting. Don't assume your content or the time you posted it will remain a secret. Be cognizant of what you post and when you post it, particularly during work hours.
4. **Laptops.** I often present in corporate conference rooms and will see eight or more people whip out their laptops to take notes. At a medium-sized conference table, that amounts to a lot of laptops and not a lot of space. Imagine 13–17" barriers between the presenter and each audience member.

This is one area where tablets are a more appropriate choice, as they're smaller and less obtrusive.

5. **Set rules.** If it is your meeting, set the rules. Ask people to mute their phones or turn them off entirely. Asking people not to take notes digitally is a stretch, but you can ask them to not check their email during the meeting.

6. **Discretion.** Sometimes, a particularly important phone call or email can warrant interruption. However, there is no excuse for a lack of communication about that interruption. If you are expecting a critical call, tell everyone about it before the meeting starts so there is no confusion if you need to excuse yourself.

7. **Keep email in its place.** Constantly checking your email on your smartphone or tablet in front of colleagues and clients will give an impression that you don't want to portray. Again, if you are awaiting a crucial or time-sensitive email, let people know. If you think you are multitasking by speaking to a colleague and typing away, you are incorrect. Your colleague may never say anything, but you can be sure they find it rude. It sends the message that the text or email is more important than they are.

8. **Email does not emote (nor does text!).** Emails are rarely seen as being too soft. Emails have no intonation, emotion, tone, gestures, or facial expressions. Remember that! Reread your emails before you send them, and if there is even the slightest chance that your email might be misinterpreted, rewrite it or pick up the phone instead. I'll share some more tips on writing effective emails in the next section.

9. **Context.** The other place where email often misses the mark and causes hurt feelings is context. You send a thoughtful, well-constructed email to a colleague. The response is, "Fine." The sender then wonders why they received a curt, short email. The responder, on the other hand, doesn't even give it another thought as he or she may just have landed, is going through a hundred emails, or wanted to reply quickly and get back to work. Without context provided, meaning can often be assumed or invented, and that rarely turns out well. When writing an email, think about the wording of your emails and how their context will be interpreted.

10. **Remote team members.** If you have a team in which most employees work on site, but one team member works remotely, then that team member is at a disadvantage. There is a certain camaraderie that forms just from working with people for hours and hours each day. In addition, there might be some jealousy around the person who gets to work from home or remotely. Make a real effort to ensure that remote team members are on site a few times per year to interact face-to-face with colleagues. Video conferences do not replace in-person interactions.

11. **Attention.** Always remember that when someone is talking to you, you should not look at your smartphone or laptop. We are all guilty of it—listening to someone, while at the same time typing or reading an email. Give the person in front of you your full attention. It matters! Trust me, people have lost jobs and important projects because of this.

Communicating through Email: Rules and Etiquette

1. **Email is formal, and it is final.** Emails last forever and cannot be taken back! Even if you try to recall a sent message, there is no guarantee that the person hasn't already read it. Email is the ultimate double-edged sword—it is so easy to use and feels so informal, yet it lasts forever and can always come back to haunt you.

2. **Read it back in court.** Don't ever think it might not happen to you. There have been plenty of cases where the prosecution or defense have used emails as admissible evidence. Before you send your email, make sure you would be happy to have it read out loud in court.

3. **Read it an hour or day later.** Emailing in anger is a definite no-no. If you ever type an email in frustration, wait and reread it at a later time when you are feeling calm before you send it.

4. **Phone and talk first.** If the subject matter is particularly important, call and talk to the person first. It is always better to discuss important matters in person or over the phone, and leave emailing for follow-up details.

5. **Print it out and proofread (attachments too) before sending.** This might waste paper, but it will be infinitely less embarrassing than a response to a request for a proposal loaded with misspellings, or an incorrectly selected attachment.

6. **You are not just representing yourself.** I would advise having a personal account in addition to a business account, and knowing when it is appropriate to use each one. The

number of times people write negative things about their boss or mention their search for new jobs—all from their business account—is unfortunately astounding.

HOW TO IMPROVE EMAIL ETIQUETTE

1. **Salutations and openings.** Again, email is formal. Nine times out of ten, a formal greeting and closing is not only advisable, but necessary. Err on the side of caution.
2. **Know your audience/mirror.** You can pick up clues as to how others process information based on how they write and respond. Pay close attention to this. I tend to try to use similar and familiar language.
3. **Subject line.** Remember, the subject is not about what you are trying to communicate, but what your audience cares about. There is an entire art to writing subject lines that will get people to open the email.
4. **Organize.** Again, organize your thoughts. Have a message, a purpose, main points, etc., just as you would with a formal document.
5. **Reply.** Very few things are more irritating than someone failing to reply or at least acknowledge receipt. I often ask for a reply or receipt acknowledgement when I send an email.
6. **Humor rule.** Sarcasm and what you think is witty might not come across as such to the receiver. Remember, your body language and nonverbal communication tools don't exist in email.

7. **Avoid writing like a tenth grader via text.** If you wouldn't put it in a proposal or RFP (request for proposal) response, I would try to avoid putting it in an email.

8. **Beware of the "reply all."** Nothing has ended more careers than an accidentally clicked "reply all."

9. **Maintain privacy/protect confidentiality.** Always err on the side of caution. If someone might not want to have his or her email address revealed, call first before you include it. Do not put other people on the spot if you can avoid it. Avoid including confidential information other than email addresses as well, whether it's yours or someone else's (see rule #2 in "Communicating through Email" on page 101).

10. **Your email is a reflection of you.** How would you handle yourself for a job interview, with a client, or with a superior? Put the same amount of thought into your self-representation when it's for an email.

ZOOM FATIGUE IS REAL: HERE IS HOW TO MASTER IT!

Chocolate chip cookies. What do cookies and Zoom have in common? Both are wonderful, in limited doses :-) When overdone, they both can make us feel pretty terrible. We all know the adage about too much of a good thing.

Zoom is quickly following the route of PowerPoint, conference calls and other unbelievably effective but oft-overused tools. Tools. Used properly, a tool is very beneficial, but when used improperly or overused, it becomes a hindrance. Ever try hammering a nail with a jigsaw?

And let's face it, Zoom can be exhausting. Yes, seeing the faces and homes of all of our colleagues felt great in Week 1,

Week 2, maybe even during Week 3. But by Week 7? And how did we end in a position where ALL calls need to be via video?

Answer: They don't. And while videoconferencing can be extremely effective, it can wear down even the most resilient individual after ten straight video meetings.

Why?

Heightened awareness and the sense of being always "on." Yes, everyone can see your face around a conference table or in a typical meeting room. But everyone is not solely fixated on you. And while they really aren't "solely fixated" on you via Zoom, it certainly feels that way, with every box neatly stacked directly in front of your eyes. Talk about raising the level of self-consciousness!

Zoom takes on the aura of a performance, and as anyone who has ever performed can tell you, that requires a lot of energy, and a lot of recovery time.

So how can Zoom be used more effectively? Here are a few ways to become more comfortable and more effective when using video conferencing.

1. **Planning.** Think back to many, many moons ago, to the good old days . . . let's say January 10, 2020. Eons ago. Think about the laundry list of meetings you had to attend. How many did you need to be physically present for? Consider saving Zoom for important calls and meetings. As with all things, too much of a good thing can have negative consequences, one of which is what we all see now—a very casual approach to calls. Use Zoom as a tool, not as the default.

2. **Agenda.** You are all dialed in, staring at each other. It is a very orderly call, until one team member interrupts another. Then another person echos the interruption. Before long, the call is off course. And just as someone is about to course-correct,

we get . . . a frozen screen. And no one knows what do to! Videoconferences are tailor-made for an agenda and a moderator/leader. It becomes unwieldy without both. An agenda will keep things focused, and also ease some of that feeling of needing to be hyper-vigilant at all times because you know what is coming next. Right now we are in a very frightening time, partly because we have no idea what comes next. We have no COVID-19 playbook to lean on. No past experience. Meetings don't have to follow the same trajectory.

3. **Relax.** Only dressing from waist-up is way too relaxed. Staring into the camera on your desktop or laptop is way too intense. Just because you are "on-video" doesn't mean you have to be on. Quick tip: when possible, turn off the view that shows you . . . you! We are all self-conscious, and having the ability to see yourself is both a) distracting and b) too rife with the opportunity to be self-critical. Don't do it. Turn off the angle (there is a cool feature on Zoom called "hide yourself"—I would highly encourage you to use it.) Focus on everyone else. It will make you feel better and will make you a more engaged participant and presenter.

4. **Just not too much!** There will be life after COVID-19. And co-workers and clients will appreciate the relaxed tone we took in terms of personal presentation during the immediate onset of quarantine. What was acceptable and even endearing in the beginning of this crisis will change over time. It always does. Be in front of that curve. And one way to do that is to . . .

5. **Dress up . . . before it matters.** I put on a button-down and jeans, and even shoes, before every video call. And not for the reason you might suspect. It is not for my audience,

although that is a nice added benefit. It is for me. The reality is that when you are dressed "for work" there is a psychological shift. This has been studied, and it makes sense.[19] And the contrarian in me says that this will actually make you more relaxed when on camera, as you will "feel" more relaxed. I would argue that "formal clothing" means different things to different people, but I would also argue that a Baby Yoda T-shirt and boxer shorts aren't considered formal anywhere.

6. **Using senses makes sense.** Smell. Taste. Touch. Three words that just begin to scratch the surface of what can get lost when communicating via video (or on the phone—for anyone under twenty years of age, that was the original purpose of the device used to access text and social media) rather than in person. The office you worked in had a certain smell. And taste. Research shows us that smell and taste are much more interconnected than we realize.[20] And even movements as small as adjusting a chair in a conference room or touching an object in a colleague's office changes an experience through the use of touch. Video conferencing makes it much harder to access those senses, and the two remaining senses, hearing and seeing, are much different as well. Staring into a tiny camera on a laptop, tablet or computer is much different than being in a conference or meeting room, and the intensity of it can be overwhelming for anyone who is not used to it. And the ambient noises in the background of a home are usually different than those in an office setting. So

---

19 Slepian, Michael L., et al. "The Cognitive Consequences of Formal Clothing." *Social Psychological and Personality Science*, vol. 6, no. 6, 2015, pp. 661–668, https://doi.org/10.1177/1948550615579462.

20 Hitti, Miranda. "Can You Smell Through Your Mouth?" *WebMD*, WebMD, 17 Aug. 2005, www.webmd.com/brain/news/20050817/can-you-smell-through-your-mouth.

three out of the five senses are much harder to access, and the two remaining senses are accessing information differently. So what do you do to be more memorable? Verbalize those senses! "Would you like a hot cup of Starbucks extra roast?" typically evokes more of a sensory response than "Would you like coffee?" We are all missing many of the sensory experiences that are no longer available. Utilizing brief sensory language when discussing topics will make them more memorable.

7. **Narrative development.** If you thought it was hard to get someone to pay attention to a PowerPoint deck with seventy-five slides, each laden with a hundred words when people met in person, good luck in this current environment. And it is not necessarily for the reason you might think, although in many cases it is :). In our pre-pandemic world, we were faced with endless distractions. Now those distractions have changed—kids zooming in classes, people you love around your workspace 24/7, neighbors walking by, the nonstop social media blitz that is even more intense than before, and the list goes on. It is simply harder to remember granular detail when that detail has so much competition. By having a clear message and building a narrative around that, the chance that your message will carry further and last with someone longer goes up exponentially.

Again, Zoom and other video-conferencing solutions are wonderful tools and I count myself as lucky to have access to them. That being said, these tools have limitations as well. Life is very, very intense at this moment in time, and a full day of video-conferencing only adds to that intensity. Utilizing some of these ideas should bring down some of that intensity, increase memorability and increase overall organizational effectiveness.

Five Teleprompter Tips

The teleprompter has gotten quite a bit of attention recently.[21] After witnessing many *faux pas*, here are my five quick tips to make the teleprompter experience a bit more rewarding for you.

1. **Always bring a physical copy of the text with you.** There is little worse than discovering that the text you thought was loaded into the teleprompter was loaded incorrectly or is otherwise not working. Remember that, as with any electronic device, a teleprompter can fail to work properly.

2. **Tennis is best left on the court.** It is often obvious when a speaker is using a teleprompter, as the speaker's head tends to turn from left to right as if watching a tennis match, when it is really moving from screen to screen. It may be difficult, but try to avoid this.

3. **Create your own teleprompter "lingo."** This would be a type of shorthand—phonetic spelling, underlining, "stressors," hyphenated pauses, etc.—inserted into the text to remind you when to pause, change your tone, lighten the atmosphere, or use a natural gesture. It is easy to lose your connection with the audience while using a teleprompter by speaking in a monotone voice with no intonation or expression. Creating your own lingo can help prevent that.

---

21 Baker, Peter. "Tales of Totus, the President's Teleprompter." The Caucus, *The New York Times*, 29 Mar. 2009, http://thecaucus.blogs.nytimes.com/2009/03/25/tales-of-totus-the-presidents-teleprompter/.

4. **Don't stare.** If you are using a single-screen teleprompter (especially if using it to record a presentation to be viewed later), remember you are talking to people and not to the machine! While eye contact is crucial, there is a fine line between constant eye contact and staring. If you are not making eye contact at all, it becomes obvious you are reading. Break your visual contact, even just for a second or two.

5. **Practice. Practice. Practice.** If you are going to use a teleprompter, practice extensively with it every time. Just because you are comfortable with it for one address does not mean you will be as comfortable the next time. Also, familiarity with the text is critical to success when using this device.

A teleprompter can be your best friend or your worst enemy in a presentation. If choosing to use a teleprompter as an aid, make sure you have practiced, so that your presentation will appear engaging, natural, and appealing to your audience.

CANON ZOOM LENS EF 24-70mm 1:2.8 L II USM
Φ82mm

CHAPTER 7

Media

The New York Times. The Washington Post. The Wall Street Journal.

ABC. CBS. NBC.

CNN. Fox News. CNBC.

Cheddar. The Skimm. The Street.

Facebook. Instagram. Twitter.

A blogger with 1,000 readers. A podcaster with 150 listeners. A YouTuber with a following of 100. An influencer with an audience of 100,000.

What do these entities all have in common? All are considered sources of news by constituencies throughout the world. The "media" used to be clearly identifiable—see the top three rows above. Now the "media" is literally everywhere. What does that mean? It means opportunity. So how can you maximize the potential opportunity? Here are some ideas to get you started . . .

Meeting the Media

Broadcast television. Newspapers. Magazines. Radio. Blogs. Social media. Online news programs.

Media across the globe have adopted many practices of the Western media, running similarly styled programming, similar show formats, and more. Uniform global media has created a great opportunity for you to be ahead of the curve in pursuing additional opportunities to represent your brand.

With the media no longer limited to broadcast television, print, and radio, every person with a smartphone is a potential journalist. Every time you or your representative speak at a conference or on a panel, there is a chance that the appearance will end up on a blog, on a website, or on a video-sharing site. If journalists are there, what would once have been a print interview may now actually stream onto a website.

This is NOT a reason to be nervous—it is actually a tremendous opportunity! It means there is a lot more potential exposure and an added opportunity for your message about the best firm in the profession to reach a much larger audience.

The key to successful interaction with the media is proper preparation.

The Camera is Never Off

The tour of your facility has ended, there were no hiccups, and now you and your "guests" are engaging in friendly banter in the parking lot. But the camera may not be off.

Whether meeting with the media or addressing an entire company, if you adopt the mindset that the camera is still rolling, not only during the event, but before and after it, you will prevent gaffes, damaging comments, and other headaches from occurring.

This media-training principle doesn't only apply to a situation when you or your staff are before the media. For instance, imagine you are the CEO of a multinational corporation conducting a video conference with thousands of employees. The conference has ended, but you are still in the room where the video conference took place. The webcam is never off.

You are a VP addressing eighty employees via teleconference—the phone is never off.

This mindset is not easy. The natural inclination—once the stress has subsided, the situation has turned friendly, casual conversation begins, and one is no longer "on"—is to engage in conversation with those around us, and for that conversation to be less guarded. It happens to most of us (and I readily include myself).

The vast majority of the time, the camera or recorder will be off, and the phone may very well be hung up . . . Unless it isn't.

MEDIA RELATIONS 101: COMMON WISDOM

Say something provocative, inflammatory, or compelling during a television taping, and it's probably going to run. Call the reporter or producer and ask him or her to pull the segment, and it will *definitely* run.

MEDIA RELATIONS 201: THE FOLLOW-UP

Calling a reporter after the fact and asking that the segment get pulled because you had a headache during the taping is not only a guarantee the segment will air, it also ensures that you will now have to deal with more stories about the phone call, a much larger audience, and most importantly, it means you lose control of messaging for a period.

Three Timeless Tips

1. Practice and prepare with your team before going on the air.
2. Learn about the intricacies of the media, and the outlet you are dealing with, prior to meeting.

3. If you say it, prepare to deal with it. Calling the reporter after the fact and making an excuse will only draw more attention to whatever you said.

Four Steps to Get from a Difficult Question to Your Answer

1. Acknowledge the question with a short answer
2. Transition
3. Deliver your message
4. Be quiet!

Examples of Transition Phrases

"Now, putting this in proper context we need to look at ..."

"Having said that ..."

"Let me put this into perspective ..."

"Let's take a look at the facts ..."

"Let's discuss the current state of the situation ..."

"The real issue here is ..."

"We asked ourselves the same thing, and that is what led to ..."

"Our main concern is ..."

"What we're really talking about is ..."

"What's missing here is the issue of ..."

"To clarify ..."

"To answer, let me rephrase ..."

"More importantly ..."

"This is what I can tell you ..."

"I don't view it that way. What I (we) see is ..."

"Your question raises an even more important point ..."

"That is not an area of my expertise, but what I can tell you is ..."

"Here at ..."

Media Preparation in 2020 and Beyond

Media has changed dramatically in the past five years, let alone the sixty years since the famous Kennedy-Nixon debates. In the sixties, or even the eighties when I was a child, television was popular—very popular. Media was powerful. All powerful. Each television channel and newspaper dictated quite a bit, and at a young age I was a reader of our local paper. My parents wouldn't allow television to be a staple in our household, much to my chagrin, but for most of my friends, the outside world was fixated on television and playing Atari.

> "We can no longer afford to be second best. I want people all over the world to look to the United States again, to feel that we're on the move, to feel that our high noon is in the future."
>
> JFK

In 2020, our options are different. Commercials aren't a necessary evil for television watchers. You can get almost any content you want, on demand, 24/7, in almost any country. There are more outlets available now than at any point in history, and new outlets are being created (at least seemingly) by the second. Some individuals have become actual "outlets" of their own.

There are millions of hours of YouTube content uploaded every hour. There are no media cycles, only media minutes, as the "Breaking News" of today would be that there is no breaking news! Content spreads, and it spreads quickly. This means that an error on television, a web channel, or anywhere else can spread like wildfire and lasts forever, but can also be forgotten by everyone except the unlucky individual involved, shortly after the public shaming has ended.

In the midst of all this change, one media principle that has remained constant is how guests and other figures who don't appear on television or in front of the public every day prepare when they do. Much of this preparation follows rules similar to the last sixty years—like how to use makeup, what colors to wear and not to wear, how to position your hands, or how to answer an unfair or unpleasant question. Certainly, much of this is still valuable, but there has been one seismic change in preparation tactics that you should factor in more than any other principle, whether you're preparing a friend or your boss (more on that in a minute).

So what is the biggest change?

Conditioning.

Virtually every person alive has been watching visual broadcasts of some form or another for most of their adult lives, and for many people, it has been their entire lives. People have now seen virtually everything. That means people are very conditioned to others' responses, and they realize, consciously or subconsciously, when a guest "bridges," deflecting a question without offering any type of answer.

We now notice when a politician doesn't even attempt to answer the question, or even states that they won't answer the question, but instead goes right to talking points. When a "political advisor" or "security expert" or anyone else is clearly regurgitating talking points they have been given.

So what? If people are conditioned, who cares? Most guests are imminently forgettable. Other than cursing and getting "BLEEPED" for saying something completely outrageous or getting very angry and/or walking off, most viewers seem to forget who the guest they saw was.

Why? I think it is because everyone looks, sounds, and acts the same. Going straight to a boilerplate message is commonplace. Talking points are commonplace. Holding your hands in one position is commonplace.

What isn't commonplace? Telling quick but effective stories. Using one syllable words rather than jargon (and every industry uses jargon). Answering questions crisply and quickly. Providing new information to audiences. Treating an interview like an interview (not a conversation you are an equal partner in). Being oneself. Being authentic. Holding yourself like you normally do. Saying something relevant and important to the individual viewer—not important to the guest, but important to the viewer.

Media Preparation Tips

HOW TO PREPARE FOR YOUR NEXT (OR FIRST) INTERVIEW

- **Do your research.** If you have staff, ask for a comprehensive briefing book with the basics—the reporter, the reporter's background, the reporter's style, the outlet, past stories, current events, etc. If you don't have a staff, you can do it yourself.

- **Prepare and practice.** Question and answer, repeatedly, with a colleague, staff, or a confidant. Don't worry about having an answer to every possible question. Focus on themes and lines of potential questioning instead (you can never predict every question)
- **Get a feel for rhythm and cadence.** How fast do you speak? How fast do you respond?
- **Do your research on yourself.** Read your own website, coverage, and old articles. It's all fair game!
- **Learn your disfluency lexicon.** What words do you use when you are nervous or under pressure? "Uhh . . ." "To be honest . . ." "In all honesty . . ." "Like" "You know" "Listen . . ."

WELCOME TO CNBC ... OR WHY WE ARE ALL CONTRIBUTORS ON CABLE NEWS NOW

What do remote media interviews and remote videoconferencing have in common?

Have you ever watched your favorite news program and wondering how they manage to have full studios in even the most remote locations and in every city, everywhere?

Answer: They usually don't.

What you are usually watching is someone sitting in a remote broadcasting studio, and more and more frequently, someone utilizing Skype or a similar platform. And there are tips and techniques that are helpful to become more comfortable in those settings.

Now we are all in that setting. Quarantining has made us all "professional" remote guests. So how do tips and techniques from media interviews translate to your next Zoom call? Let's dig in:

1. **Turn off the television or your camera.** You are a guest on CNBC talking about your business. But you aren't in New York. You are in Des Moines, entering a downtown office building, inside of which is a satellite studio. You exit the elevator onto the third floor where you are escorted to a nice enough room with a camera (maybe more, depending on the setup), a chair or two and one or two television sets placed on either side of you. And that's it.

   You are now mic'd up, the earpiece placed in and you sit. And now it's just so. And then you are told you are on in 5 . . . 4 . . . 3 . . . 2 . . . And there you appear, live on CNBC, with a backdrop of beautiful Des Moines talking to millions of people you can't see, while you watch . . . yourself?!?

   Staring at a camera with no or few humans around, knowing you are broadcasting to the world, is tough enough. Watching yourself in real time while you do it? BRUTAL! So what to do? Turn off the televisions so you can focus on what matters . . . the questions being asked from NYC and your answers coming from Iowa.

   Now take down the stakes (but only in your head). You are in your office/living room/kitchen/child's bedroom getting ready to "Zoom" with your team and your leadership. Same situation. They are somewhere other than in your physical presence. And you are looking at yourself, and doing what? Judging! How do I know? We all do it! And studies show us that most of these thoughts are a) repetitive and b) negative. So what can you do about it? The same thing you can do if you are on CNBC. Turn off the camera YOU can see!

2. **Seven seconds of death . . . or why live isn't live.** We've all seen it. A host asks a question to a guest or reporter on your favorite news program. The guest/reporter is somewhere far

away. The question is asked . . . and then . . . nothing. Every second feels like an eternity to the viewer. And then a second or two later, the guest answers . . . either as the host is asking another question, or fairly delayed.

Now let's head to your favorite weekly conference call. You ask a person, let's say Matt, a question. And . . . nothing. Silence. After a few seconds of very uncomfortable silence, you start to move on. But alas, all of a sudden you hear . . . Matt. Why didn't you hear him before? Because he was fumbling to turn off "mute." (And he is guilty as charged!) And that is what I like to call the "seven seconds of death." These are the few seconds that feel like eons between when a question is asked and someone tries to get off mute! The solution: if you are a moderator, slow down the line of questioning and provide the person, in every situation, a second or two to respond. If you set the tone for every questioner, that occasional latecomer won't feel so aloof. And if you are THAT PERSON (and we all have been), realize we are all pretty poor at multitasking—we think we aren't, but studies sure suggest otherwise.[22] Keep that finger by the mute button like that big promotion depends on it . . . it might!

3. **Chairs are for sitting** . . . unless you are Johnny Knoxville on Jackass! Rolling around isn't cool—check out chair options.

   You are watching your favorite broadcast investigative question a guest. They are sitting on typical office chairs, that are oh so comfortable. The chairs swivel, they have wheels for easy mobility, and are relaxing—much like the chair many

22 Bradberry, Travis. "Multitasking Damages Your Brain And Career, New Studies Suggest." *Forbes*, Forbes Magazine, 20 Jan. 2015, www.forbes.com/sites/travisbradberry/2014/10/08/multitasking-damages-your-brain-and-career-new-studies-suggest/.

of us sit in every day. And the guest is comfortable. And the questions get tougher. And the guest starts twisting and turning, adding not only to the appearance of being less than comfortable but actually causing said guest to lose a bit of grounding. Not a great look, and an even worse feeling.

Videoconferencing works in the exact same way. Having just finished my 1,000th Zoom call of 2020, I have seen more twisting and turning that you see at the Tour de France. Keep a foot rooted on the ground. Not only will it prevent distracting movement, it will increase your comfort. You will feel more rooted and more confident. Why? Simple. You are more grounded. Trust me, it works.

4. **No one can see you sweat . . . but everyone can hear you chew!** Live television. Host: "So, Congressman, what do you think about Eventoff's proposal to make public speaking part of school curriculums?" Congressman: "It's great, I support it and I think that Eventoff is doing a great job." Cut to commercial. And the camera is off, or so the Congressman thought. Congressman: "It's about time Eventoff got off his rear end and did something. He is pretty worthless." We have all seen this play out on our screens fairly regularly in the last decade.

   Good news! Or perhaps this is bad news. You don't need to be a Congressman to have this happen to you! It happens on Zoom thousands of times a day (unofficial estimate). And that might not even be the worst of it. Like listening to yourself go to the bathroom? How about someone else? Dislike when people chew loudly? When you eat while on Zoom, and your line isn't muted, the closest sound to compare it to is the March of the Orcs from Lord of the Rings. For instance, Apple makes sure you can hear it in all its glory with the ability for AirPods to capture everything.

Hint. Once you figure out how to sign in to Zoom, master the mute and video buttons before all else. They are your friends. Good friends. Great friends.

PASSPORT
United States
of America

CHAPTER 8

Intercultural

Rules often change when crossing borders. It is thanks to the huge global platforms—in the form of social networks, video and instant, immediate communication tools that work across borders—that we now have a better idea about how other cultures communicate. It is definitely a good start, but in my mind, it's just that—a start. It is imperative to be able to relate to people where they are, and that means understanding communication styles and customs that are different than your own. While in no way comprehensive, this chapter will get you started on your intercultural communication journey, with some fun activities along the way!

What the World Can Teach Us All About Communication

The world is not flat, and this is news to . . . absolutely no one! Portuguese explorer, Ferdinand Magellan, proved that the Earth was not flat almost six centuries ago. Perhaps a less well-known fact is that communication styles are not flat either.

There are always communication "commonalities," regardless of location, background, or culture. For instance, a message is essential to communication in any language, in any location.

Understanding your audience and the needs of your audience is crucial, whether you're in Detroit or Damascus.

I have had the good fortune to work with executives and leaders in over ninety countries, and from over a hundred countries. For many of them, English was a second language, and for some it was even a fourth, fifth, or sixth language.

There was a period of time when public communication never spread past the city of a company's headquarters. There was also a period of time when the leader of a private company could exist for a long, prosperous career and have limited or even no interaction outside of the executive team. But this isn't true anymore. Times have changed, and they have changed quickly.

The West has taught the world much about communication, but there is also much that we can all learn from the rest of the world.

1. **Courteousness.** During a lecture with executives in Japan, not once did someone look at their smartphone or banter with a fellow attendee—a regular occurrence with any U.S. audience. I am as guilty of this as anyone. Western audiences are courteous, but there is courteous, and then there is *courteous*. In some instances courteousness is cultural, in some it is due to interest, and in others it is just expected. The advent of "smart" devices has created a distracting effect on audience members, and while a speaker might be ineffective at delivering his or her message, it doesn't mean that it's acceptable to be impolite.

2. **Open-mindedness.** I often present in a way that is completely different than what an audience is used to. I involve the crowd, walk around, and create an interactive setting. In Japan, I'm often described as being extremely "genki," which means enthusiastic and energetic. In the West, people can

sometimes cast a skeptical eye toward someone imparting information in a way that's different, but this doesn't seem to happen in other locales. The desire to learn allows for the temporary withholding of judgment. Instead of finding my approach strange and intimidating—and becoming noticeably indifferent as a result—audiences suspend disbelief and always (and I mean *always*) at least provide the benefit of the doubt when trying what I suggest. I find no reluctance to try something new, even from those who were asked to practice my methods in front of their peers. That is not an easy thing to do, and it usually takes a bit more urging to get similar-sized groups in the West to do the same.

3. **Supportiveness.** Presenting can be scary, and presenting in a second language even more so. Each participant is always given the chance to immediately utilize the techniques they learned, and everyone always participates, though it is not an easy or comfortable thing to do for anyone, and is even more intimidating in a second or third language. Yet each and every speaker had the full attention, encouragement, and support of the audience. It was nothing less than amazing. The peer support made all the difference. Western audiences are just as supportive of each other, but often do so in a quieter way, which is counterintuitive.

4. **The power of the pause.** One side note, albeit an important one, is that trainees tend to report that they think in their native tongue. This makes sense. Not every word has a translation, and trying to think and translate at the same time is extremely onerous. I often work with simultaneous translators and am amazed by their ability.

   What this forces bi- or multilingual executives to do, especially when responding in English-speaking interview situations (media and board interactions come to mind), is have a built-in pause. While a slight pause is often accepted regardless, those who have to cross a language barrier may pause a few seconds longer than a native speaker. Those extra few seconds are a gift, as they allow the speaker to gather their thoughts. But something else invariably happens in that pause as well. The speaker is usually more comfortable and secure in his or her answer. There is less disfluency (and there is disfluency in EVERY language). Answers tend to be more compact, with more clear and concise messaging.

This reinforces just how valuable and important the power of the pause is, even for those of us who do not have to translate from a native tongue.

5. **Feedback.** I have my own style of providing feedback, which I believe is effective, encouraging, and empowering. It is very considerate of the receiver of the feedback, and it has proven successful for two decades. One thing it typically isn't is harsh—until that was actually requested, like it has been over, and over, and over again, in many European countries. The desire for tough feedback, typically areas for growth rather than positive reinforcement, is different in different locales. Feedback that would be considered tough or harsh is usually expected in parts of Europe. That same feedback would cause major problems in the United States. That feedback would get me sent home in some Eastern countries, while it is clearly desired in some MENA countries. The world is not flat.

Empowering students and future leaders with the tools necessary to communicate effectively not only makes for a stronger home country, but it also benefits the world. In a world that effectively grows increasingly smaller as technology advances, the opportunity to interact and share information is crucial to our mutual success—because as famed writer Robert A. Heinlein said, "When one teaches, two learn."

How to Communicate Effectively Across Borders

The world hasn't really grown smaller. The number of miles or kilometers between Dubai and Detroit is the same as it was a century ago. It may take less time to get from Point A to Point B, but the world is not shrinking as much as it may seem to be.

The barriers to working across countries and between cultures have decreased. To grow in our global economy, every business has to think beyond its borders. It's vital. Those with effective cross-cultural communication skills will be among the most successful of the 21st century. Those who fail to acquire them will be left behind.

While norms and customs vary, there are many universal characteristics of effective public speaking that transcend borders. Here are ten tips you need to know:

1. **Slow down.** The pace of the average speaker tends to speed up when he or she is in front of an audience. In a normal conversation there are periods of pause, but the sound of silence is usually left out of the rapid cadence of question and answer. Slow down when speaking in front of an audience to ensure that you are understood.

2. **Enunciate.** Clearly hitting all syllables prevents words from colliding into one another. Paying proper attention to

enunciation allows your audience to clearly hear and process every word. It will also slow you down.

3. **Adopt the customs.** When communicating across borders, especially when visiting, take time to learn local customs. I often consult a local expert before a meeting to learn about culture, history, and key words and phrases. People are generally friendly, so if you don't know, don't be afraid to ask.

4. **Learn some of the language.** To illustrate respect and effort, I would argue that it's almost imperative to know key greetings, words, and phrases before an initial meeting. There are literally hundreds of websites and applications that can help with this. I try to use three or four audio apps to practice pronunciation.

5. **Think *two-for-one sale.*** Listen more than you speak. While this is by no means a scientific calculation, I try to listen twice as much as I speak when interacting with a new colleague in a culture that is unfamiliar to me. I do this so that I can focus on language as well as gestures, facial expressions, and what is happening around me. It has the added benefit of slowing me down and allowing me to be fully present.

6. **It is not about you.** You are a guest, even if you are the guest of honor. Use "you" and "we" more than "I" and "me." This is especially important in cultures that tend to be more collectivist, where the frequent use of "I" and "me" may send a message that you do not intend to send.

7. **Do not let one interaction cloud your judgment.** We tend to stereotype different countries and cultures, and much of it is baseless. Think back on the preconceptions you've held in your life. How many were proven incorrect?

Do not let one interaction set up your frame for the entire country; instead, learn from it. I've worked in more than sixty countries and have seen grace as well as rude behavior in each and every one.

8. **Learn what is taboo.** In a business setting, talking about politics, religion, or sexuality will probably lead you somewhere you don't want to go, no matter the location. Inserting your opinion about local behavior, political situations, or religion often sends a message that will not work in your favor.

9. **When in Rome.** Expressions have many different meanings. A thumbs-up is a positive sign in the United States, while in other countries, putting your thumb up will garner dirty looks. A thumbs-up with an open palm might even get you punched in Greece.[23]

10. **Colloquialisms.** Every country has local expressions and phrases. Those colloquialisms don't necessarily translate well. Remember that in your interactions. I find that colloquialisms actually cause more misunderstandings than anything else on this list, except for misuse of humor and lack of listening.

11. **Strive for clarity.** Clearly communicate questions, as well as your expectations for answers. Never assume someone holds your perspective. Summarize what you think was implied in a conversation. "Yes" can mean "I agree" or "I understood the question" or simply "I acknowledge what you said."

12. **Humor isn't always funny.** Humor and sarcasm do not necessarily translate well, and they can both get you into "hot

23 In Greece, a thumbs-up with an open palm is called a "moutza" and is a gesture to offend, similar to the middle finger in the United States. Its origin dates back to the Byzantine Empire.

water" in "short order." Similarly, metaphors, colloquialisms, and expressions may not translate well, may make no sense, or worse, may convey something rude or inflammatory. Keep this in mind before you go in for the laugh.

The bottom line is this: "Si fueris Romae, Romano vivito more; si fueris alibi, vivito sicut ibi." If your Latin is rusty, this phrase means, "If you are in Rome, live in the Roman way; if you are elsewhere, live as they do there." Jeremy Taylor, a cleric in the Church of England, said those words in 1660, and they're just as true today.

QUICK POP QUIZ:
Body Language around the World

QUESTIONS

1. In what country does a head nod mean "no"?
2. What does thumbs-up mean in Germany?
3. What does the "OK" sign mean in France?
4. What do fingers crossed mean in the USA?
5. What do fingers crossed mean in Vietnam?
6. What does showing the sole of one's foot mean in the Middle East?
7. What does "Hook 'em horns" refer to in the United States?
8. What does "Hook 'em horns" refer to in Italy?
9. What does spitting mean in China?
10. What is the meaning of a one-handed presentation in Japan?
11. What does the typical "come here" motion mean in the Philippines?
12. What does a hand up mean in the United States?
13. How about a hand up in Greece?
14. What does thumbs-up mean in West Africa?
15. What do fingers crossed indicate in Vietnam?

ANSWERS

1. Bulgaria
2. One
3. Zero
4. Good luck
5. An obscenity
6. Disrespect
7. Fans of the University of Texas
8. Your spouse is cheating!
9. Nothing, just spitting! (Not considered rude)
10. Rude; presentation of cards or items should be with both hands, out of respect
11. Disrespectful
12. Stop talking; talk to the hand
13. Disrespectful
14. Obscenity
15. Considered rude

EXIT

CHAPTER 9

Crisis

This is a hard chapter to write and one we hope you never need to refer to after you have read and digested it. Unfortunately, odds are you probably will. Crises are a fact of life and a central part of business. Missed earnings, resignations, down cycles, layoffs, stalled fundraising (especially for startups), offshoring, and board shifts all have the potential to turn a minor issue into a major disruption. And some have the potential to turn into very damaging internal and external crises. Read the front page of any paper or turn on the news for ten minutes, and it's likely that you will see a company in some form of crisis. And unfortunately, many of those companies are woefully unprepared. But yours doesn't have to be. This chapter is a starter kit to get your crisis juices flowing and give your team some resources to start pulling together. Rule number one of all crisis communication—fail to plan, plan to fail! So let's start planning . . .

Protect Your Reputation

An unfortunate reality of life is that crises occur, and they often occur when we least expect them. Few organization are hit with a crisis on a Tuesday afternoon at 2 p.m. when things are a bit slow and all hands are on deck. So what are some steps your organization can take to prepare today for a potential crisis?

1. **Start planning now.** Plan and prepare before you think you need to. What are your organizational themes when you are not in crisis mode? Identify your key messages. Who is on the messaging team? What does your organization stand for when there is no crisis? What is your organization known for? What are your organizational weaknesses?

2. **Crisis response/Crisis communication plan.** You must have a written crisis response/communication plan. I often ask executives if their organization has a crisis response plan, and the answer is almost always "Yes." Then, I ask if they know what is in it. At this point, the "Yes" gets a bit more sheepish. I also ask if they have reviewed it in the past six months, and this is when the nervous laughter begins. Make sure to create your plan ahead of time, review your plan regularly, amend your plan continually, and ensure that every key member of your core team is intimately familiar with the plan.

3. **Assemble your direct crisis response/communication team ... today.** Determine roles, the chain of command, and crisis command posts, all before the crisis comes up. Trying to figure out these roles and responsibilities while you are in full crisis mode can really put the organization in a precarious position. Who is in charge of what? Who manages the existing business? Who reaches out to customers who have yet to be affected? Who reaches out to regulators? Who contacts employees? Who reaches out to neighboring businesses? Who is in contact with the community? The media? The list goes on and on, and you should make sure yours is complete.

4. **Assemble your professionals.** Public relations professionals, communication specialists, industry experts, compliance

professionals, public affairs professionals, outside counsel, audit teams, and crisis experts should be on auto-dial. Identify and interview key consultants when things are quiet, and develop your relationships with them today. Waiting and then identifying key professionals during a crisis is much more difficult and expensive. Doing so allows for limited or no time to get them up to speed on your business and situation. It also allows for considerable time to pass and the crisis to escalate.

5. **Determine internal communication protocol.** Who will be responsible for communicating internally to ensure that no one is "talking outside of school?" What is the process for disseminating information throughout the organization? If you do not communicate internally, you can rest assured that your employees will, and chances are, you will not be happy with what they are saying and telling others. Any person who has a touch point outside of the organization (which is everyone), has the potential to deliver a message externally that contradicts the organizational message. This usually happens because no one told that individual what was occurring or how the organization plans to respond.

6. **Voice.** Who is the voice of the organization? Is there more than one voice? Should it always be the CEO? (Answer: it depends.) How many lines of business is the company involved in? Who communicates internally? Externally? Who ensures that your business continues to operate even as the crisis develops?

7. **What do you say?** Do you say anything before you know anything? Saying, "No comment" says a lot more than no comment at all. This is where preparedness training, drills, and live simulations really help to prepare key executives and

spokespersons for the real thing. What if there are reports of injuries? How are you receiving information? There will be a lot of incoming requests for information. How will you reach out to stakeholders?

8. **Stop and breathe.** Practice putting yourself into semi-stressful positions through crisis-response drills. Warning—this is absolutely not a substitute or representative of how you will feel like in the middle of a crisis. But it will prepare you by giving you tools to work with during an actual crisis, such as knowing how to breathe properly to control both epinephrine and your heart rate.

9. **What does the filtration system look like?** In a crisis, there may be a number of parties who want answers about what is going on within your company. Who filters each call and determines who answers which questions? What are the answers for those questions?

10. **Who is monitoring social and web media?** What is the process for answering questions and comments online? What does the strategy look like? Whose responsibility is this? In today's day and age, ignoring the power of social media is a mistake. There are a number of excellent social media crisis communication professionals, so having contact with one is never a bad idea.

11. **Opposition research.** In political campaigns, not only do campaign teams research the opponent, but they also research their own candidate to determine what might "pop up" at the most inopportune time. Do a comprehensive internal "opposition research" report on yourself—what else might come to light in the face of a crisis? What are your answers

to the questions that might arise? What else should be on your radar screen?

12. **Inside/Outside.** Do not forget to communicate internally! This point is important enough to mention twice. How you handle yourself during a crisis sends a strong message to your employees.

13. **Spokesperson.** Make sure your spokesperson is trained and media ready. This is one area in which on-the-job training never works! Being a spokesperson in the midst of a crisis is a brutal job to begin with. Doing so with no preparation is not only unfair, it is unwise and will hurt your organization.

14. **Pay attention to borders.** If you are a multinational organization or you operate internationally, think about how a crisis abroad would affect your business here. Again, what are your answers? Who is doing the answering? Recent corruption allegations against major multinationals—that occurred thousands of miles from U.S. borders—still got a lot of media attention in the U.S.

A Crisis Doesn't Always Mean (News) Coverage

When companies communicate internally through a crisis, there is no such thing as a one-size-fits-all (or one-solution-fits-all approach). Every day there are myriad stories in the news about companies dealing with crisis situations, and you can be sure that many more never make the news.

Crises can cause damage to your company, but that damage can be minimized if the organization enjoys good relations with its investors and employees beforehand.

RELATIONS WITH THE BOARD AND INVESTORS

There are clear, concrete steps every business leader can take to ensure that communication with a board or investors is much more effective during down cycles or quarters. While not a secret formula, these steps can help prevent a minor crisis from escalating in scope or an internal situation from becoming a very public external situation.

1. **Develop relationships with board members and investors BEFORE bad news or a crisis hits.** Sometimes board members are the best advocates a company can have during a tough quarter. One of the keys to having effective advocates is regular contact and flow of information, both with the board and with investors.

   This is why some of the greatest political leaders of our time continue to make phone calls and write notes to key supporters during off years—long before election season is looming on the horizon!

2. **Communicate more often.** There is a tendency (when times are good and everything is running well) to communicate a little less about happenings within the company. But this is the time to communicate more! Don't reserve communication for monthly meetings—especially during tough economic times. Yes, a CEO wants to spend as much time as possible "adding value," but keeping investors and board members active, involved, and included (rather than frustrated) adds as much value as anything else.

3. **Pick up the phone.** Call your investors and board members regularly. They might be too busy to take the call. Call anyway. They may tell you that you do not need to call. Call anyway. Remember back from Chapter 3 . . . Your voice matters!

RELATIONS WITH MEMBERS OF THE ORGANIZATION

At the same time, the last thing any executive wants or can afford is to only focus on investors and board members. What's equally as important is communicating regularly throughout the organization. An organization in which every member has a sense of loyalty and belonging will react much more cohesively in a crisis situation. This cohesion can be encouraged by following these communication tips:

1. **Be open, be available, and talk to people.** Myriad divisions can often breed a small-team atmosphere. If you are the CEO or a leader in your organization, be seen. Get out there, talk to people, and, equally important, listen to people. Employees who are heard and seen will be far more likely to have your back the day a crisis hits if they feel like you have theirs every other day.

2. **Treat your top talent as your most precious asset.** If you think you have listened to them enough, go back and listen to them one more time. If you are not communicating with your top talent and letting them know they are heard and appreciated, they are looking elsewhere. Replacing superstars who have been headhunted is not easy.

3. **Develop a message.** Your organization needs to know not only what is going on, but what it means. This is the message. How does what you do, or what your team does, further the efforts of the organization? How does it help the business achieve its bottom-line objectives? You MUST be able to clearly articulate the value of your position to the organization. This often takes time and effort, but it is crucial. Make the investment.

4. **Be consistent.** Nothing deflates an organization or a team more than perceived inconsistency in communication or communication style.

5. **Be open with information.** Access to information is an essential part of morale-building within an organization. Be open with information, let people know what is going on, and allow them to feel like they are part of the organization. This is all part of successful communication.

6. **Never try to hide the bad news.** This a) is no longer possible and b) will destroy all credibility. It is always better if the CEO, for example, delivers the bad news than if it is delivered by someone outside the organization.

7. **Be first.** Define the news before anyone else defines it for you. This is politics 101: if you have negative news or news that could be construed in a negative light, communicate it first. If you don't and something negative exists, someone will find it. This is one game in which finishing second does not lead to a silver medal!

Crisis Rules for CEOs

Takeaways for CEOs, whether Fortune 100 or startup:

- The microphone is always on, as is the camera—okay, maybe not literally, but certainly figuratively. CEOs of public companies know this well, but the rule holds just as true for every private company. Every word you say is open to analysis and interpretation and no longer has a shelf life. If you say it, you own it. Once-private events can become public in an instant.

- You are NOT an individual! If you are the CEO, you aren't a private citizen. Like it or not, every time you speak, you speak for the organization. Your thoughts will be reported along with your title, and the title is what makes it newsworthy.

- Power is more fleeting than ever; no matter how popular a CEO is, a damaging statement can undermine that popularity and the power that comes with it. Today's nearly instant communication and messaging allow that statement to get away, like an old-school game of telephone. It is often very unfair, but it happens. That unfairness and unpredictability can cause CEOs to ask, "Why bother?" when it comes to spending resources building and protecting a public persona. But those investments will pay off, as they can decrease recovery time when a crisis occurs.

- Time. Unfortunately, there is not always a way to bring a crisis to a quick conclusion, and getting caught in the firestorm can be brutal. While time might not heal all wounds, it does heal many. A solid strategy and the passage of time can help with the rebuilding process.

- How you respond to the crisis and set the tone for the day will often be more important than the crisis itself. Identify your key audiences, put yourself in their shoes, and communicate to them directly (which is not always as easy as it sounds).

CHAPTER 10

Students

I was a student once (shocker), and more often than not, I wasn't even a very good one. Throughout my days as a student, I had many interviews, and since then, I have conducted many, many more. The process of interviewing is changing through the use of video, and it will change even more in the future. At the same time, many aspects will stay the same, as long as interviewing involves human beings with heartbeats and emotions and thoughts and feelings.

Every year, I prepare many, many students for what will be a very important interview in their lives: a job desperately wanted, a fellowship within reach, or an internship that might change the course of their life. Each interviewee and interviewer are unique, and it is impossible to provide personalized advice in a book chapter. However, there are things that ring true for everyone. Read on to find a number of interviewing principles to consider. And don't stop there. I will show you how to rock that internship once you get it, too!

Interview Basics: Fifteen Reminders

The most important thing to remember when preparing for your interview is to *be yourself*! In this day and age, it seems like every student has straight As, perfect test scores, and has saved millions of lives in remote lands . . . Okay, I'm exaggerating a bit, but you get the picture. As a student, there is a lot of pressure to be someone extraordinary.

However, if what you say in an interview isn't the truth, or if it's an exaggeration, you will not be able to pull it off—I promise you that. Authenticity and sincerity go further than you might realize, so be true to yourself and to who you are. This does not mean you need to be overly humble, but it does mean you should stay true to your character and values. Do not apologize for who you are. Be proud of who you are!

DAYS AND WEEKS BEFORE

1. **Practice interview questions and answers.** Since grade school, you've probably heard that practice makes perfect. And while it might not make you perfect, what is true is that practice makes you significantly better. Guess what: LeBron James practices. Peyton Manning practices. Former President Barack Obama practices. Even Beyoncé practices. So before your big day, why wouldn't *you* practice?

2. **Identify points to remember.** What are your key talking points and the information you want to make sure you mention? Both remembering and mentioning them will come naturally with practice. Reflecting back on an earlier conversation and thinking, "I wish I had remembered to say . . ." is all too common. Spend some time thinking about the most important things that you want someone to know about you!

3. **Do your research and become intimately familiar with the school or organization to which you are applying.** If you are unprepared when interviewing with a

university, you might say the following . . . "This is a great institution with great values. My father, mother, sister, brother, and grandparents all went here. I can get a great education." But what do these statements have in common?

They are the most frequent responses in college interviews, and they won't make you stand out! What your family has done is irrelevant. The institution wants to know about *you* and your specific interest in them.

Differentiate yourself. Learn about the school to which you are applying, its programs, what they are known for, professors you would like to study under, groups you would like to join, etc. Make sure what you say is memorable by thoroughly researching and becoming familiar with the subject matter.

DAY OF THE INTERVIEW

4. **Dress how you wish to be perceived.** What that means is, if you want to present yourself as Ivy League material, don't dress like a college dropout. Just like if you were to run for president, you'd make sure to look presidential.

   This may all sound like common sense, but it needs to be said: shower, brush your hair, clean and trim your fingernails, iron your clothes, and shine your shoes. That's a start. Next, make sure your socks don't have holes in them, your shoes don't look old, and your briefcase or purse isn't falling apart. Shirts should be tucked in. Clothes should match. If you aren't the most fashionable person, ask someone who is! You do not need to look like a model, but you do need to be clean and dressed appropriately.

   If you don't personally own the appropriate clothing, don't fret. Many universities have programs that provide clothes for interviews at significantly reduced prices, or that are even free, and friends or professors can likely lend a hand as well. There is no excuse!

5. **Arrive early!** Ending up in the interview room drenched in sweat because you were running late is never a good idea. So unless you *literally* live around the corner from the location, try to arrive thirty minutes early to avoid surprises and allow yourself time to focus on the task at hand.

6. **Remember, as soon as you appear on location, your interview has begun.** Obviously, you don't know everyone on campus. The person in the bathroom, the individual passing you in the hallway while you're on your cell phone, and the individual for whom you do or do not hold the door open could all be the person who will be interviewing you. You never know! Be careful about what you say and do while on campus. Running into your interviewer beforehand actually happens more often than you'd think.

7. **Turn off your cell phone.** There is nothing more distracting or rude than a cell phone going off during an interview. Vibrating is not much better. Whether it's your phone ringing or an alert that you have a new text message, don't let it happen—make sure your phone is off. If the person interviewing you does reach for his or her phone or is texting, that is not an indication that you should as well.

INTERVIEW TIME

8. **Make eye contact.** When you meet your interviewer, look that person straight in the eye and be ready to shake hands firmly. When he or she is speaking to you, look at them directly. Don't dart your eyes around the room or avoid his or

her glance. If a group interviews you, look at the person who is speaking to you, and then try to make eye contact with each person in the room as you respond (as long as you do not "ping-pong" back and forth).

9. **Smile.** This one seems easy, but it often isn't. When you meet someone and introduce yourself, smile—genuinely. Ask them how they are doing, and wait for a response.

10. **Watch your posture.** I know, I sound like your mother, but you should keep your shoulders back and spine straight when you enter the room. Wait for your host to sit first. Once you sit, make sure your back stays straight (do not slump). Practicing with a friend or teacher before the interview can help identify how you sit under pressure. To help keep your energy up, try leaning forward about five to ten degrees.

11. **Root into your heels.** Rocking back and forth, up and down, or tapping is distracting. Depending on how you normally sit, putting your weight on one or both of your heels can help keep you still.

12. **Listen before formulating your response.** Most of us begin to formulate a response to a question before hearing the entire question. Not only does this lead to a misunderstanding about what is being asked, but it also often results in speaking before the interviewer has finished! So . . .

13. **Remember: L-P-A (Listen – Pause – Answer).** The easiest way to root out disfluency (umm, ahh, like, you know) is to follow this rule. Really listen to the question and take time to process what is being asked.

Then pause for a second or two before answering. This short silence shows that you are really thinking about the question. Now answer. It's always better to have a well-thought-out and articulate answer than a speedy one.

14. **Ask at least one question yourself.** There comes a time in every interview when you have an opportunity to ask questions. The interviewer may or may not ask you if you have questions, but you should ask one anyway. This is where your research beforehand puts you in an optimal position. Ask educated, focused, school-specific questions—they will help you stand out as a candidate.

AT ALL TIMES

15. Remember your manners (please and thank you). Do not chew gum immediately before, during, or after the interview. Always send a follow-up "thank you" email.

21 Interview Questions You Should Master

1. Why do you want to go to this (high school, college, university)?
2. Why do you want to work at/in ________?
3. What do you bring to this school/position/job title?
4. Tell me about yourself.
5. How do you plan to make a difference here?
6. What is your greatest strength?
7. What is your biggest weakness? In what area can you improve the most?
8. What accomplishment(s) are you most proud of?
9. What do you plan to do after graduation? What is your goal after this position?
10. Who do you look up to? Who are your role models? Why?
11. What has been the most challenging experience you have had? How did you overcome it?
12. What is your favorite subject? Why? What is your favorite part of your current position? Why?
13. What is your least favorite subject? Why? What is your least favorite part of your current position? Why?
14. Tell me a story that would define who you are as a person.
15. What are your hobbies? What do you tend to do outside of school/work? Please elaborate.
16. What do you like to read outside of school/work? What is your favorite book?
17. What teacher or mentor has had the greatest impact on you? Why?
18. If you do not get into ________, what is your plan?
19. Where else are you applying? Why?
20. If I forgot everything about you except for one thing, what would be the one thing that you would want me to remember?
21. Do you have any questions for me?

Rock Your Next Internship: Communication Tips for Interns

Internships have made a huge difference in my professional growth, and I believe they are fundamental in learning how to handle yourself in the professional world. I have at least two paid interns year-round and advise many, many more on how to go about pursuing and excelling at internships.

There are a lot of ways to successfully pursue an internship and maximize the opportunity once you have received it. Four cornerstones that every summer intern should remember to maximize at every opportunity are summed up in an acronym: DEAL. The acronym stands for:

Differentiate ... and deliver

Employer-focused

Ask questions

Lose the ego

- **Differentiate.** There are some tasks that every individual can do extremely well. There are others that everyone can do well enough. Differentiate yourself by greeting every person you meet on the job, regardless of title or position. Say hi to the cleaning crew. Know their names. Address your superiors with proper salutations. Ask people lower on the food chain to serve as informal mentors. Say please and thank you. Stay a little late to help someone who is not your boss. These things all help you to stand out.
- **Employer-focused.** Everyone knows the old adage, "What's in it for me?" Change your thought pattern, and instead, ask:

What's in it for my employer? How can I help them (over and above what I am already doing)? How can I add unexpected value?

- **Ask questions.** You don't necessarily need to ask probing questions, but questions, especially those about how people rose to the positions they are in, are valuable. What advice they have for interns just starting on career paths. How the business you are working in works. How the person you are working for got in the business. Questions lead to gaining insight and experience you simply can't get from a book, and they help you build a deeper connection and relationship with those you work for.
- **Lose the ego.** I have had some pretty lousy experiences as an intern and early on in my career—cutting and pasting newspaper clippings for hours on end wasn't a lot of fun. If someone asks something inappropriate of you, says something offensive, or asks something illegal of you, report it immediately. But if someone asks you to make photocopies when you feel you should be in the boardroom, lose the ego. If someone asks you to rewrite a document, but you act as though you shouldn't have to, it's not going to be a summer where you develop long-standing relationships. Lose the ego and realize your superior might be right.

CHAPTER 11

ABCs

As Simple As ABC: What Leaders Can Learn From Masterful Orators of the Past

There are so many noble causes led by charismatic, effective leaders, yet it is difficult for many of these leaders to establish a clear message that resonates and connects with the audience. This isn't due to the content or quality of the cause, but because we are all subject to information overload.

However, masterful orators have succeeded in every generation. One factor that has not changed over time is the ability of a master orator to captivate and move audiences, and to attain levels of success that many thought were unachievable at the time. Each of them did so because they mastered the ABCs of communication.

THE ABCS: ACTION, BREVITY, AND CONVICTION

Long before you learned to read or write, you needed to master your ABCs. Communication is no different. Before you can create an effective message or master the details of public speaking, body language, gesturing, and more, you must master the cornerstones, or the ABCs, of communicating and messaging.

Over the past decade, ease of access to information has grown exponentially, and the speed at which it travels has become blinding. Today, we have access to more information than we could have possibly imagined a short time ago—and there is likely more of it available than a human being could ever want or even need. We have entered an information age in which today's front-page story is literally "yesterday's news." So how do you make sure your voice is distinguished from all the others? What are the secrets of master orators?

There are countless books written on communication, public speaking, and presenting—many with very good advice and some semblance of practicality. These books are read, re-read, and widely discussed. However, something important is missing from many of them.

What do successful messages have in common? What do those who have delivered these messages have in common? They all follow *the ABCs of communication*—which is, unfortunately, often an overlooked thread woven through all of the great speeches and presentations.

Put simply, Sir Winston Churchill did not use PowerPoint. Franklin Roosevelt did not put on slideshows. Abraham Lincoln did not have the media of television and radio available to disseminate his message to the masses. However, these leaders still reached widespread audiences, both in and beyond their times, by mastering basic, fundamental communication principles, starting with the ABCs.

A) ACTION (A CALL TO)

Chances are quite good that a leader wants to move an audience. He or she wants to motivate, persuade, or influence the people to do something, i.e. take action. This idea of doing something can range from taking physical action (volunteering, protesting, advocating, demonstrating, or letter writing) to action that is less physical (voting) to something that is not physical at all (changing a thought process, goal, desire, or in some instances the course of life itself).

President John F. Kennedy's Inaugural Address has been one of the two most frequently published addresses in the last sixty years. The most famous statement in the address is:

"And so, my fellow Americans: ask not what your country can do for you; ask what you can do for your country. My fellow citizens of the world: ask not what America will do for you, but what together we can do for the freedom of man."

It is remarkable how powerful these lines were, not only when they were originally delivered, but also now, six decades later.

In fact, President Kennedy's daughter, Caroline Kennedy, sees this call-to-action as one of the greatest legacies of her father. When describing the inspiration for the John F. Kennedy Profile in Courage Award, she notes:

> *"Ever since I was a little girl, people have told me that my father changed their lives. They got involved in public service, in government, in their communities because he asked them to and they wanted to be part of something larger and better than themselves. President Kennedy's inaugural challenge—'Ask not what your country can do for you; ask what you can do for your country'—inspired a generation in the 1960s that transformed our nation with courage and dedication and in turn inspired those who followed. To me, that is one of his greatest legacies, and it is in them that his spirit lives on."* ~ Caroline Kennedy, *TIME* magazine, 2007

Why was President Kennedy's speech so effective? It turns on the fact that it was a call-to-action. People didn't just hear the speech only to have it slip from memory; the closing call-to-action left those who heard it with a lasting sense of meaning and responsibility. In fact, some found the speech so enduring that the Sixth Floor Museum at Dealey Plaza—the museum that chronicles the assassination and legacy of President Kennedy—hosts a special exhibit entitled "Call to Action."

B) BREVITY (SIMPLICITY)

Quotes throughout history have emphasized the benefit of brevity when speaking or presenting in public. From Roman statesman, scholar, and orator, Cicero, who stated, "Brevity is the best recommendation in speech, whether in a senator or orator," to President Franklin D. Roosevelt, who said, "Be sincere; be brief; be seated," brevity while speaking has long been viewed as a virtue.

No better example of brevity exists than President Abraham Lincoln's Gettysburg Address. Numerous books have been written about this famous address, and presidents throughout history have studied its words. The first six words of the address, "Four score and seven years ago," are ingrained in every elementary school child's memory in America. Though many facts surrounding the address have been debated, two have not.

First, Abraham Lincoln was not the keynote speaker; Edward Everett, a sought-after orator of the day, was. Edward Everett was considered one of the greatest orators of his time, and he had been designated as the keynote speaker for the dedication of the Gettysburg monument. Second, Edward Everett's speech was over 15,000 words long and lasted over two hours, while Lincoln's Gettysburg Address was 272 words long and lasted between two and four minutes.

Edward Everett quickly recognized the virtue of brevity, commenting to the President after hearing his speech, "Mr. Lincoln, if I could have come as near striking the keynote of this occasion in three hours as you did in three minutes, I should be better satisfied with my performance."

Today, the Gettysburg Address is revered as one of the greatest speeches ever delivered. President Lincoln is often regarded as one of the greatest leaders in U.S. history, and Edward Everett's name is barely known. Why? While it is not possible to study the cadence, tone, or delivery (areas on which Everett likely focused) of a speech given nearly 165 years ago, the words behind the speech itself still remain.

President Lincoln was able to deliver so much power in his address not in spite of its brevity, but because of it. There was no time for his message to get diluted, for his thoughts to twist and turn, and for his audience to lose their focus. The President was able to grab the audience's attention immediately and hold onto it. No superfluous words, no unnecessary sentences, and no dilution of message. Brevity seized the day then, and brevity will seize the day now.

C) CONVICTION (CHARACTER)

> *"He wasn't a natural orator, not at all. His voice was raspy. A stammer and a lisp often marred many of his speeches. Nor was his appearance attractive . . . Short and fat, he was also stoop-shouldered."*
>
> ~ Thomas Montalbo, DTM, *Churchill: A Study in Oratory*

Add to that Sir Winston Churchill's quick sarcasm and strong opinions—characteristics that were certainly not universally liked or accepted—and you begin to wonder how Churchill was able to persuade and influence so effectively.

Churchill used his conviction to will not only his whole nation, but also the entire world, to change course. The sheer will and conviction of Churchill, his words, and his beliefs may have been just as beneficial to the British cause as the logic of Churchill's argument, his credibility, or his emotional appeal.

One can argue that the "We Shall Fight on the Beaches" speech was also a call-to-action—and it was. This speech can be and has been studied and utilized to demonstrate how to give a speech, how to use repetition, and a host of other "how tos." While the speech offers something for everyone, what specifically does it offer a leader today? It offers evidence of the power of conviction when speaking or presenting a message.

Listening to "We Shall Fight on the Beaches," one can feel the raw power, feeling, emotion, and drive in Churchill's every word. Churchill had railed against the Nazi regime, often without an audience and long before it was in vogue to do so. When opinion turned, there was no questioning his conviction. It is hard to imagine a British citizen not being inspired upon hearing the final paragraph of this inspiring address:

> *"We shall go on to the end, we shall fight in France, we shall fight on the seas and oceans, we shall fight with growing confidence and growing strength in the air, we shall defend our Island, whatever the cost may be, we shall fight on the beaches, we shall fight on the landing grounds, we shall fight in the fields and in the streets, we shall fight in the hills; we shall never surrender, and even if, which I do not for a moment believe, this Island or a large part of it were subjugated and starving, then our Empire beyond the seas, armed and guarded by the British Fleet, would carry on the struggle, until, in God's good time, the New World, with all its power and might, steps forth to the rescue and the liberation of the old."*

His conviction never wavered, even when he was not in power. This was evident in his communication to the British Empire's citizens, her allies, and her enemies.

So what? What does this information mean to the leader of a company, whether it has two employees or 20,000? Or to a not-for-profit leader trying passionately to motivate or attract supporters? Or what is the significance of conviction to a political candidate running for a local or federal office?

Chances are, barring some unforeseen circumstance, the vast majority of leaders will never: a) have to communicate to as large an audience as a president or prime minister does; b) have the resources available that a world leader does; or c) have the ability to reach the masses through paid or earned media the way a world leader does.

So how can a leader utilize the ABCs of communication effectively in light of what we've learned above?

A) ACTION

A speech or presentation given without a call-to-action is a speech or presentation not worth giving. I have come to the conclusion after years of experience that if there is no desired action or reaction on the part of the speaker or presenter, there is very little reason to speak or present at all. The list of potential actions a speaker may desire is endless: support, opposition, motivation, dissuasion, encouragement, education, organization . . .

In order to utilize this principle effectively, I believe the best course of action for a leader to take is to ask him- or herself prior to developing a talk, presentation, speech, meeting outline, or press conference to answer the following three questions—as they are fundamental in both determining the message and the message's effectiveness:

1. What do I want to accomplish? What do I need the audience to remember if they only remember one thing?
2. What is the desired result? What do I want the audience to do?
3. Who cares? Why should they care?

These questions, with proper introspection and preparation, will lead the speaker to develop a message with a clear call-to-action.

B) BREVITY

Once a basic message and call-to-action have been determined, the hard work of deciding exactly how to develop and deliver this message begins. Determining what words to use, how to phrase them, how much detail to give, and how much information to provide are the logical next steps. Once you have ascertained what you are trying to accomplish, you need to figure out how to accomplish it. And in communication, there is no substitute for brevity.

In the vast majority of presentations (speeches, debates, press conferences, announcements, etc.), the one universal similarity is the tendency to include more information than is necessary to convey the message. This frequently leads to message dilution or to the message getting lost completely.

Look to advertisers, or more importantly, copywriters and newspaper editors, and now online "clickbait" headlines, for excellent examples of how to use extreme brevity to attract attention. Newspaper and magazine headlines are created with one of two purposes in mind. Either a) get the customer interested enough to purchase the publication, or if the publication doesn't require purchase, b) get the customer to read the article following the headline.

While never as brief as a headline, a leader should utilize brevity in order to whet the appetite of the audience, communicate a core message, or get the audience interested in the subject and desiring more information—all leading to the generation of action.

Leaders can use the cornerstone of brevity effectively by answering the three questions in the "Action" section above, and then asking what information is absolutely necessary to elicit the desired action or reaction. The most effective way to do this is through preparation, practice, and the effective "whittling down" of content until the core message and crucial information is all that is left. For more instruction on developing a message, refer back to Chapter 2.

As famous French writer Antoine de Saint-Exupéry (author of *The Little Prince*) said so eloquently, "Perfection is achieved, not when there is nothing more to add, but when there is nothing left to take away." Every leader should think about his or her communication in the same light.

C) CONVICTION

The perfect call-to-action, with the perfect amount of information, delivered in perfect fashion, will still fall flat if the audience does not believe that the speaker believes in what is being communicated. Of the three cornerstones, conviction is, at its core, both the simplest and the most difficult one to implement. That simplicity and difficulty both stem from the same place—within the speaker.

It is the simplest because it is either there or it is not. It is the most difficult because it cannot be learned or faked. A leader either strongly believes in his or her message or doesn't. There is one thing every leader should realize: an audience can sense how much conviction is behind a message.

So how can a leader effectively utilize conviction?

Put simply, make absolutely certain that you believe in what you are about to say prior to saying it. No amount of practice or preparation will help a leader convey conviction if he or she simply does not fully believe in what he or she is communicating.

ABC) AUDIENCE

Again, most leaders will not have the opportunity to reach the masses in the way that a president or prime minister can. But that makes the utilization of the ABCs even more critical.

While everything a president says and does is closely scrutinized, chances are if he or she has an "off day" or misspeaks, he or she will also have the opportunity to rebound and "message correct" in the future. The audience will still be there.

There is a strong possibility that if a regular speaker fails to connect and communicate a message effectively, even once, the chance to reach that same audience may not come again. This makes it crucial to invest the time to determine clearly what your message is, to be able to capture and communicate that message as simply and briefly as possible, and to make sure that prior to communicating this message you feel confident and believe in the message you are about to deliver.

You may not be able to reach the number of people that a president can, but the opportunity exists for leaders to spread their messages well beyond the limitations that existed before. Barriers to sharing information are being torn down all around us, making it possible to reach not only those you know already, but also those who may have an interest in your cause or company continents away.

There are so many voices out there clamoring to be heard—you may not get a second chance if you lose their attention.

So you must master and follow the ABCs. They are the cornerstones and building blocks of all successful communication.

In an age where technology changes the way in which we communicate each and every day, the alphabet still exists as the bedrock of the English language, the very foundation of our words, and the basics with which we formulate thoughts and opinions. The same holds true of the ABCs of communication. No matter the technology, medium, venue, audience, or audience size, there is simply no greater way to achieve communication success or convey a message effectively than by following your ABCs.

Every time you prepare for a presentation, try out different methods, and learn what works best for you. I have been presenting for many years and I am still learning every day. As technology changes, so will our need to adjust our patterns of communication. Who knows, maybe you'll be the next great orator who will be written about in books to come!

Appendix A: The List

Unlike a traditional "reading list" at the conclusion of this book, I wanted to offer something for everyone—articles that will help you grow as a presenter. Rather than just offer a list, I wanted to add a bit of color to what you will be reading, so there are takeaways from each speaker. So start thumbing through, figure out what you might want to learn more about, start your exploration, and enjoy!

I. The Gaffe

I would be remiss if I didn't discuss one of the biggest "fears" I hear on a daily basis: the dreaded gaffe. Forgetting what you might say, tripping on the dais, saying something incorrectly . . . the list goes on and on.

I train and prepare executives to deliver speeches, presentations, panel appearances, and more, and I have watched thousands of presentations. If I have not seen it all, I have at least seen quite a bit. When it comes to presentations, one person's gaffe may be that same person's big opportunity (although he or she may not know it).

The illusion of transparency (discussed in Chapter 1) is also applicable when it comes to gaffes. Your "major gaffe" might actually not even be picked up by your audience. When it comes to public presentations, everyone always fears the gaffe—but in reality, it should sit very low on your list of worries.

I have seen many people emit strange sounds—tummy rumbles, odd intonation, dramatic and inappropriate pitch changes, strange word (or non-word) choice—and the audience reaction is always the same: a smile, maybe a quick laugh, and then right back to listening mode. In other words, it has no real, lasting effect on the people who matter (the audience), only on the person who doesn't (the presenter). Pro tip: a gaffe can also make you more relatable (and therefore memorable), so it can actually work in your favor. I know, this is totally contrarian over the long term (welcome to my world), if handled properly (which means keep on going).

The biggest gaffe when it comes to a presentation isn't a fumble, it isn't freezing, and it isn't emitting some odd sound; it is being completely unmemorable. If audience members don't remember the core of what you said (your message), don't remember you, and can't articulate what you were talking about an hour after your presentation (a very common occurrence), then that is a gaffe to be concerned about. And that gaffe is preventable through preparation, practice, and numerous other strategies and tactics.

That being said, we are all human . . . So when strange sounds emit, we feel we made an odd movement, or we simply freeze, what should we do? I can tell you what I do. I acknowledge it with a little smile and slight self-deprecating remark ("I'm not quite sure where that came from . . ." or "Ouch, brain freeze . . ."), and I keep moving forward. The key is to keep moving forward. Don't dwell, don't apologize, don't make fun of yourself (again, a very, very light self-deprecating remark—not multiple remarks!), and keep going.

II. The Twenty-Three-Year-Old Who Changed Communication

Winston Churchill, as you'll know if you've already read through this book, is widely revered as a great orator. I have written about him often, as he has been a hero of mine since childhood. When one searches for books about Winston Churchill online, the list seems endless, and there are dozens and dozens of books containing his published speeches alone.

Churchill was not only a legendary orator; he was also a prolific author of both fiction and nonfiction. His final collection, *A History of the English-Speaking Peoples*, is a must read.

With Churchill being both an author and an orator, it should be no surprise that he wrote one of the most important and impactful works on oratory and public speaking. It is five pages in total, and it was never published. "The Scaffolding of Rhetoric" was written by a twenty-three-year-old Winston Churchill while he was stationed in India. It has been preserved and is available for all to read due to the generosity of the International Churchill Society.[24]

In "The Scaffolding of Rhetoric," a young Churchill delves into the importance of oratory and the power that it can bring, starting from the first sentence ("Of all the talents bestowed upon men, none is so precious as the gift of oratory . . .") and continuing to build on that foundation. Churchill's conviction should be no surprise to anyone who has read about Churchill's hero, the great Orator W. Bourke Cockran. Congressman Cockran and his oratorical skills influenced Churchill from an early age.

---

24 "The Scaffolding of Rhetoric," The International Churchill Society, https://winstonchurchill.org/publications/finest-hour/finest-hour-094/the-scaffolding-of-rhetoric-2/.

It is impossible to do "The Scaffolding of Rhetoric" justice in a short article. Churchill covers so many principles, and while the essay is only five pages, I discover something new each time I read it. It is still amazing to me that it was written by Churchill at age twenty-three, and that the vast majority is as relevant in 2020 as it was in 1897.

Some key gems:

> *"Rhetorical power is neither wholly bestowed nor wholly acquired, but cultivated."*
>
> *"Before he can inspire them (his audience) with any emotion, he (the orator) must be swayed by it himself."*
>
> *"Before he can move their tears his own must flow."*
>
> *"He may often be inconsistent. He is never consciously insincere."*

Those gems are all from one sequence. The treatise builds and contains thoughts on presence, diction, rhetorical devices, messaging, structure and so much more. Again, this is a must read for anyone who communicates—which is everyone!

III. The Most Famous 272 Words in History

> "Four score and seven years ago our fathers brought forth on this continent, a new nation, conceived in Liberty, and dedicated to the proposition that all men are created equal.
>
> Now we are engaged in a great civil war, testing whether that nation or any nation so conceived and so dedicated,

can long endure. We are met on a great battlefield of that war. We have come to dedicate a portion of that field, as a final resting place for those who here gave their lives that that nation might live. It is altogether fitting and proper that we should do this.

But, in a larger sense, we cannot dedicate—we cannot consecrate—we cannot hallow—this ground. The brave men, living and dead, who struggled here, have consecrated it, far above our poor power to add or detract. The world will little note, nor long remember what we say here, but it can never forget what they did here. It is for us the living, rather, to be dedicated here to the unfinished work which they who fought here have thus far so nobly advanced. It is rather for us to be here dedicated to the great task remaining before us—that from these honored dead we take increased devotion to that cause for which they gave the last full measure of devotion—that we here highly resolve that these dead shall not have died in vain—that this nation, under God, shall have a new birth of freedom—and that government of the people, by the people, for the people, shall not perish from the earth."

~ *President Abraham Lincoln*

There are some key public speaking and communication lessons that everyone—whether in a boardroom or on a blog—can gain from studying this remarkable address.

1. **Be brief.** While there is always debate surrounding the Gettysburg Address, this much we know—the entire address was under 300 words and took less than three minutes to deliver. Think about that next time you address your board,

your constituents, the jurors, or the venture capitalists from whom you are requesting $15 million.

2. **You are *always* the featured speaker.** The keynote speaker on November 19, 1863, in Gettysburg was not Abraham Lincoln. It was Edward Everett, who spoke for nearly two hours; Lincoln was an afterthought.[25] If you are introducing someone or closing an event, treat it as though you are the featured presenter. This means that even though you might not be the "main event," practice as if you were. You never know, history might prove that you were!
3. **Simple word selection works.** Try to avoid 100-point Scrabble words, fancy jargon, or acronyms. Lincoln's word choice was clear and effective—accommodating every listener's education level.
4. **Paint a picture when you speak.** While not always referenced as such, the Gettysburg Address is a story. Lincoln used his words to paint a picture of this story. It is an aspirational story, with narrative development (the opening—where we have been), a hero (or heroes—the brave men and women), a vision, a seemingly insurmountable obstacle, and a way to overcome that obstacle. In under two minutes.
5. **Motivate.** The Gettysburg Address provides clear direction as to what Lincoln wanted listeners to do—show support for what was, at the moment he spoke, a (very) shaky government.

---

25 Malcolm, Andrew. "Happy Birthday, Gettysburg Address." Hot Air, 20 Nov. 2010, https://hotair.com/archives/latimestot/2010/11/20/happy-birthday-gettysburg-address/.

Does this mean that if a blog post is over 300 words, or a speech takes over two to three minutes, that it is ineffective? No. It means that when speaking or writing, focus on what the audience really wants and needs to know, rather than just on what you want to say. Brevity usually wins.

IV. The Speaker History Should Never Forget

William Bourke Cockran may be one of the greatest speakers of all time. Who is William Bourke Cockran, you ask? And, how can I make such a bold statement? After all, I never witnessed him speak, as he passed away long before speeches were recorded on video.

Since I was a young boy, I have been fascinated by the ability of an individual to influence through spoken word. I am often asked which orator has had the biggest impact on me, and my oratorical role model is Sir Winston Churchill. And who was Churchill's oratorical role model? William Bourke Cockran.[26]

William Bourke Cockran, a congressman from New York City in the early 1900s, was described in his day as the greatest orator in the land. He also served as an oratorical role model for a young Winston Churchill. It was not just Churchill who held Cockran in such high regards as an orator—it was the vast majority of his peers.

The sad fact is that William Bourke Cockran might be the greatest speaker whom no one knows about today. Books on him are few and far between, with my favorite being *Becoming Winston Churchill: The Untold Story of Young Winston and*

26 "William Bourke Cockran." *Wikipedia*, Wikimedia Foundation, 31 Dec. 2020, http://en.wikipedia.org/wiki/William_Bourke_Cockran.

his American Mentor, written by Michael McMenamin and Curt Zoller. There are not many online resources dedicated to Cockran, and even his *Wikipedia* entry is lacking.

Cockran was noted for his ability to move colleagues and constituents to support causes or even change positions due to his magnificent oratory.

Churchill once wrote to Cockran about Cockran, saying, ". . . there are few more fascinating experiences than to watch a great mass of people under the wand of a magician . . ."

Congressman Charles O'Brien (district of New Jersey), said the following at Cockran's memorial service:

> *"Much has been said and written about his ability as an orator. For ages to come, his will be the standard upon which men of similar genius will be judged. In all the history of the world, no man has surpassed and few have equaled him."*

Finding information about Cockran might be difficult, but there are clear lessons that young Churchill and many other leaders learnt from him. Here are a few:

1. **Rhythm.** Every speech should have a rhythm although most don't. Cockran was known for his rhythmic speeches.

2. **Presence.** Cockran knew the power of presence and used his body, gestures, and voice to captivate and move the audience. So can you—no matter your body type, height, weight, or voice. You can use your best qualities to your advantage. Everyone has natural strengths; it's just a matter of finding them.

3. **Conversational language.** Every presentation or speech is a conversation—both verbal and nonverbal. Use your language and body language to affect the audience.

4. **Power of delivery.** It's not only what you say, but also how you say it. Deliver your speech with confidence! Did you know that people who speak well are perceived as more competent, trustworthy, and knowledgeable?

5. **Subject matter expertise.** Cockran was not only known for his oratorical skill, but also for his mastery of the subject upon which he was speaking. So be an expert or really understand what you are speaking about. It's much better to talk about a subject you understand than just to memorize a speech.

V. Speakers Can (and Do) Change The World

On August 28, 1963, Dr. Martin Luther King, Jr. delivered his "I Have a Dream" speech from the steps of the Lincoln Memorial. This seventeen-minute address is an amazing oratorical display.[27] Very few people will ever address an issue as important (with the whole world watching); however, everyone can learn valuable lessons about presenting from this speech. Here are a few:

1. **Cadence.** King's control of cadence is simply amazing. No words are lost, and key pauses exist throughout the entire address. One technique to try to learn cadence is to read great speeches along with the soundtrack of the person delivering it.

2. **Rhythm.** Great speeches have great cadence and great rhythm. This speech had both.

27 "Martin Luther King Jr. I Have a Dream Speech." *American Rhetoric*, 20 Aug. 2020, www.americanrhetoric.com/speeches/mlkihaveadream.htm.

3. **Inflection.** During this speech, King used inflection to clearly stress certain different words. With the proper use of inflection, there should be no confusion in the audience as to which point you are trying to make.

4. **Eye contact.** King read quite a bit of his speech, but when he reached crucial sections, he looked right at the 200,000 people watching him.

5. **Rhetorical tools.** King used *anaphora*—repeating a sequence of words at the beginning of neighboring clauses, thereby lending them emphasis. For example, "I have a dream . . . I have a dream . . ."

6. **Passion.** Is there any question whether King felt every single word as he delivered it? While your presentation may not be on a subject as personal or important to you, there needs to be something that you feel strongly about around the subject matter. Find it.

7. **Practice.** It is rumored that King went off-script at the end of this address. However, it is also rumored that he practiced the vast majority of this address extensively prior to delivering it. Chances are, you are probably not as orally gifted as King, so if he had to practice, you should practice too.

> "A speech reminds us that words, like children, have the power to make dance the dullest beanbag of a heart."
>
> **Peggy Noonan**

Remember, a speech is poetry: cadence, rhythm, imagery, and passion!

VI. The Author who Changed Public Speaking

George Orwell, public-speaking expert? There is little doubt that George Orwell is one of the greatest literary minds of the 20th Century, and that his legacy continues into the 21st century, and likely for generations to come.

Best known for literary hallmarks (and required reads) *Animal Farm* and *1984*, Orwell, born Eric Blair, was not only a prolific author. During his lifetime, which ended tragically at the age of forty-six, Orwell was a political activist as well as a producer for the BBC.[28]

> "It's a beautiful thing, the destruction of words. Of course the great wastage is in the verbs and adjectives, but there are hundreds of nouns that can be got rid of as well."
>
> **George Orwell, *1984***

Orwell published numerous works, but there is precious little that would define him as a public-speaking expert. So can Orwell be categorized as such?

The secret lies in an essay Orwell wrote in 1946, entitled "Politics and the English Language."[29] This essay, at that time a call-to-action against poor political writing and the decline of the quality, and impact of the written modern-English word, is widely read, is taught in many classrooms and is revered by many authors today.

28 "George Orwell." *Biography.com*, A&E Networks Television, 16 Jan. 2020, www.biography.com/writer/george-orwell.

29 Dag, O. "George Orwell." *George Orwell: Politics and the English Language*, www.orwell.ru/library/essays/politics/english/e_polit/.

The essay teaches many lessons, and concludes with six rules that are not just rules for the written word, but are just as significant for the spoken word. The rules are:

1. Never use a metaphor, simile or other figure of speech which you are used to seeing in print, metaphors that are overused or of which the meaning is no longer clear.
2. Never use a long word when a short one will do.
3. If it is possible to cut a word out, always cut it out.
4. Never use the passive where you can use the active.
5. Never use a foreign phrase, a scientific word, or a jargon word if you can think of an everyday English equivalent.
6. Break any of these rules sooner than saying anything outright barbarous. (Barbarous: very rude or offensive; very cruel and violent)

George Orwell was not the only legendary communicator who held some of these beliefs. Sir Winston Churchill often wrote about brevity in communication, including in some official papers to staff.[30] Mark Twain once concluded a letter with,"I didn't have time to write a short letter, so I wrote a long one instead." The Gettysburg Address, one of the most iconic speeches ever given, consisted of 272 words in total, of which 204 were one syllable.

30 The National Archives. "Churchill's Call for Brevity." *The National Archives Blog*, The National Archives, 17 Oct. 2013, blog.nationalarchives.gov.uk/churchills-call-for-brevity/.

VII. The World Waited Over Twenty-Five Years to Hear These Words

Nelson Mandela's life, legacy, and contribution to humanity will be studied for generations to come. Mandela's skill as a wordsmith and communicator will also be studied for generations to come.

Whether in his longer address at the opening of his trial fifty years ago in 1964, or in his statement upon his release from prison in 1990, Mandela clearly understood the power of words and language.

The sentences that Mandela closed with, both prior to imprisonment and upon his release, were carefully chosen, extremely powerful, and symbolize why he is one of the most revered figures in modern history. The final lines clearly articulate his message:

> *"During my lifetime I have dedicated myself to this struggle of the African people. I have fought against white domination, and I have fought against black domination. I have cherished the ideal of a democratic and free society in which all persons live together in harmony and with equal opportunities. It is an ideal which I hope to live for and to achieve. But if needs be, it is an ideal for which I am prepared to die."*
>
> *April 24, 1964*
>
> *February 11, 1990*

Mandela is certainly one of the most effective orators in modern history. His contributions to oratory and public speaking are many. Here are seven:

1. **Message development.** When reading or listening to a Mandela speech, it's clear that his message is well constructed, audience appropriate, and consistent.

2. **Expression.** Nelson Mandela was masterful at utilizing his facial muscles for emphasis whenever he spoke. His smile could light up any room, and served as a huge highlighter when delivering key lines. I am always particularly moved by his eyes—at some points when he speaks, even on a video clip, it often seems that he is looking directly at you. Which leads to . . .

3. **Presence.** Mandela carried himself like a man twenty years younger than his age. When speaking, it was clear he knew the power of nonverbal communication—he stood straight, shoulders back, no swaying, no rocking. He spoke with a measured cadence, and utilized pausing effectively to emphasize key points. Before he spoke, it was clear that a leader was on stage.

4. **Perfection.** One of the first lessons would-be orators can learn from Mandela is that no speaker is perfect. No speaker. Some of Mandela's speeches were quite long and occasionally he would read directly from a script for long stretches with little eye contact. Yet Mandela and his speeches are routinely included in lists and books citing great historical speakers and speeches.

> "When a man has done what he considers to be his duty to his people and his country, he can rest in peace. I believe I have made that effort and that is, therefore, why I will sleep for the eternity."
>
> **Nelson Mandela, 1994**

5. **Rhetorical devices.** Like legendary orators who came before him, Mandela artfully utilized rhetorical devices to support his messaging. Examples of devices include metaphor, anaphora, allusion, and repetition.

6. **Quotations.** One of the greatest gifts that Mandela has left future orators is a treasure chest of powerful, impactful quotations to open or close a speech or presentation, or to utilize to support key messages. The Nelson Mandela Centre of Memory offers an entire book of his quotations.

7. **Word selection.** Nelson Mandela clearly understood the power of words and language. In a world where public figures often discount the power of word selection, Mandela clearly knew that many, many people were listening closely to every word he spoke. His address upon release from prison illustrates Mandela's respect for the power of word selection.

As he stated when closing the 13th Annual International Aids Conference in Durban in 2000:

> *"It is never my custom to use words lightly. If twenty-seven years in prison have done anything to us, it was to use the silence of solitude to make us understand how precious words are and how real speech is in its impact on the way people live and die."*

VIII. The Best Speech of this Young Century

Malala Yousafzai addressed the United Nations and delivered what can only be described as the best speech of 2013, as well as the most powerful address of this decade (so far).[31] Malala Yousafzai is a great global communicator.

31 Salass, Nader. "Malala Day At UN: Teen Activist Shot By Taliban Said 10 Moving Things That Gave Us Goosebumps (VIDEO)." *HuffPost*, 6 Dec. 2016, www.huffpost.com/entry/malala-day-at-un_n_3586266.

She was sixteen years old when she was shot in the head at point-blank range in Pakistan. Malala was shot because she wanted to . . . learn.[32] And she was a young woman. A young woman who wanted to learn.

The goal of the shooting was to silence her. The result was the creation of an inspirational advocate for global education who has the ear of the world.

Malala Yousafzai is an exceptional public speaker, period. Not a young speaker. An exceptional public speaker.

There are lessons for all of us in Malala's famous address. There are over twenty public-speaking lessons for every executive, political, academic, and professional presenter. Here are just a dozen:

1. **Practice.** Malala knew that for this one moment in time, the eyes and ears of the world would be focused on her. She was not reading text for the first time. She was not "winging it." There is no question that Malala had practiced the speech countless times. It showed.

2. **Preparation.** There are too many powerful lines to mention. That is because the preparation that went into this address was extensive, and there was no extraneous information. Malala knew this was her opportunity to deliver a powerful message, and prepared with that in mind.

3. **Message development.** There was no mistaking what Malala's message was. It was not buried in facts, details or statistics. It was relevant, actionable, repeatable, enduring, and relevant (the RARER method).

---

32 Ali, Iftikhar. "They thought bullets will silence us, but they failed : Malala on Malala Day at UN." *myglobalcommunityday, WordPress*, 13 Jul. 2013, https://myglobalcommunitytoday.wordpress.com/2013/07/13/they-thought-bullets-will-silence-us-but-they-failed-malala-on-malala-day-at-un/.

4. **Call-to-action.** In fact, several direct calls-to-action. "We call upon . . ." was at the beginning of six sentences.

5. **Pausing.** There was no disfluency in Malala's address. None. Why? Malala employed strategic pausing that helped to root out disfluency, and also added to the power of her delivery.

6. **Chunking.** Malala was delivering from a written document (I am unsure if it was a prepared text, or notes), but only spoke while looking down once. Instead, she looked down at her written document, captured a "chunk" of what came next, paused, looked up, and delivered it.

7. **Eye contact.** By utilizing "chunking," Malala was able to make eye contact with the entire body of the United Nations for the majority of her presentation.

8. **Rate.** Malala's rate of delivery was perfect. The speech was written, and delivered, with the audience in mind.

9. **Volume/Pitch.** Again, a great example of the proper utilization of both volume and pitch.

10. **Inflection and enunciation.** It was clear where Malala wanted the stress to be on each word. Each word was crystal clear.

11. **Rhetorical devices.** Metaphor, anaphora, repetition, polysndeton (One child, one teacher, one book and one pen), triads (Mohammed, Jesus Christ and Lord Buddha. Martin Luther King, Nelson Mandela and Mohammed Ali Jinnah) are but five examples. This speech will be studied for some time to come.

12. **Power.** The power and determination on Malala's face, and in her voice, was amazing.

July 12, 2013, was not only Malala Day. It was an important day in the world of public speaking and oration. It was the day that the world was introduced to a great global communicator.[33]

IX. How "the greatest" Became "The Greatest"

Although not the original "greatest." Muhammad Ali is a boxing legend and historic figure. He's also one of the most fabulous showmen to ever live. His speaking style—including his wit, amusing quips, and flamboyant statements—is easily recognizable. But you might be surprised to learn that it's not entirely his own.

Ali was nineteen when he met "Gorgeous" George Wagner, a professional wrestler from the sixties. Known for his thick, platinum-blond hair and his charismatic personality, Wagner was a crowd favorite of sorts—audiences loved to hate him. That's because he'd get in the ring and try to incite the crowd with taunts.

Here's how Wagner described his own match on a Las Vegas radio program: "I'll crawl across the ring and cut my hair off! But that's not gonna happen because I'm the greatest wrestler in the world!"

Wagner left quite an impression on Ali who said: "I saw 15,000 people comin' to see this man get beat. And his talking did it. I said, 'This is a gooood idea!'"

So he borrowed it. Ali was a master of spin. Like Wagner, America's hatred was exactly what he wanted because it made for publicity and mystery.

33 A transcript of the entire speech can be found online at www.guardian.co.uk/commentisfree/2013/jul/12/malala-yousafzai-united-nations-education-speech-text.

At the time, the Civil Rights Movement was slowly empowering African-Americans. From Rosa Parks' refusal to give up her seat on a bus to Martin Luther King's soaring, open-air speeches, the changes were coming through gestures and talk.

What Ali did was repurpose and rebrand the oratory. It was true "trash talk"—relentless jokes, dogged jibes, quips and threats—which could blossom within a climate where lynching had taken place within living memory. Violence was cheap and disposable, but words meant power.

Ali took facets of what he saw from Wagner and incorporated them into his own distinct style. The rest is history.

I have yet to meet a person who has crafted a speaking style entirely in a vacuum. We can all identify elements of presentation styles that we like as well as styles that make us uncomfortable or simply don't work for us. The best way to improve your speaking is to closely examine elements of the styles you like and introduce facets of them into your own style. Just make sure you practice the new "recipe" long before you make it public. The stage, podium, or conference center is not the time to experiment with a new technique without prior practice.

To develop your signature style, I believe another legend, Bruce Lee, said it best: "Absorb what is useful, discard what is not, add what is uniquely your own."

Then you can be the greatest—albeit not the original greatest.

Appendix B: Rhetoric

Rhetoric is an abused word. Rhetoric is NOT people just saying empty things. We constantly hear on television, or see in articles, or hear in conversation, that what he said, or she said, was ". . . just a bunch of rhetoric." Oh, how we all wish it was!

Rhetoric is an ancient art of discourse, and we all use rhetorical devices, or tools, often unconsciously, throughout the day. It is impossible to read the front page of a major news daily without seeing some in the headlines! There are many excellent books on rhetoric, beginning with Aristotle's *Rhetoric* circa 4th century BC (sorry, no videos available . . .). While not an easy read, it will make you a better speaker and a better writer. Below you will find some examples of a few different rhetorical devices to get started. You will also find two of the most famous speeches of the past century with devices identified, and the opportunity for you to find more on your own.

ALLITERATION

The use of words beginning with or containing the same letter or sound.

> *". . . the poison we must purge from our politics . . ."*
>
> ~ Senator Barack Obama

ANAPHORA

Repetition of words at the beginning of consecutive phrases.

> *"We shall go on to the end . . ."* ~ Sir Winston Churchill
>
> *"I have a dream . . ." "Let freedom ring . . ."*
>
> ~ Dr. Martin Luther King Jr.

ANTHIMERIA (VERBING)

Taking a noun and turning it into a verb.

Googling
Tweeting
Amazoning
Texting

ANTHROPOMORPHISM

Giving non-human beings human characteristics.

The camera loves you
The trees called to him
The wind screamed

ASYNDETON

Consecutive words or phrases linked together WITHOUT conjunctions.

"We shall fight . . ." ~ Sir Winston Churchill

"Go back to Mississippi, go back to Alabama, go back to South Carolina, go back to Georgia . . ." ~ Dr. Martin Luther King Jr.

CHIASMUS

Corresponding pairs that do not follow the typical a-b; a-b; instead they follow a-b; b-a:

"It is not the end of the beginning; it is the beginning of the end. Freedom requires religion; religion requires freedom."

~ Mitt Romney

(BASIC) CONTRASTS

Beginning – End; Sharp – Dull; Win – Loss

"Never was so much owed by so many to so few."

~ Sir Winston Churchill

EPISTROPHE

Repetition of words at the end of consecutive phrases.

> *"...Yes we can ... Yes we can."* ~ President Barack Obama

> *"... You'll see me ... You'll see me."*
> ~ Ghost of Tom Joad, *The Grapes of Wrath*

HYPOPHORA

Asking a question (rhetorical) and immediately answering it

> "So what is a hypophora? A hypophora is a rhetorical device ..."

ONOMATOPOEIA

Words that resemble the sounds they make

> *Splat*
> *Bang*

POLYSYNDETON

Consecutive words or phrases linked together WITH conjunctions.

> *"Send lawyers, guns and money."* ~ Warren Zevon

Famous Speeches

On the following pages, you will find transcripts of two of the most powerful speeches in United States history. A few examples of the use of rhetorical devices have been identified for you. Many more exist in each speech. Try to uncover as many as possible.

SPEECH 1: DR. MARTIN LUTHER KING JR.[34]

I Have A Dream

August 28, 1963

Five score years ago **[allusion]**, a great American, in whose symbolic shadow we stand today, signed the Emancipation Proclamation. This momentous decree came as a great beacon light of hope to millions of Negro slaves who had been seared in the flames of withering injustice. It came as a joyous daybreak to end the long night of their captivity.

But one hundred years later **[anaphora]**, the Negro still is not free. One hundred years later, the life of the Negro is still sadly crippled by the manacles of segregation and the chains of discrimination **[metaphor]**. One hundred years later, the Negro lives on a lonely island of poverty in the midst of a vast ocean of material prosperity. One hundred years later, the Negro is still languishing in the corners of American society and finds himself an exile in his own land.

So we have come here today to dramatize a shameful condition. In a sense we have come to our nation's capital to cash a check. When the architects of our republic wrote the magnificent words of the Constitution and the Declaration of Independence, they were signing a promissory note to which every American was to fall heir. This note was a promise that all men, yes, black men as well as white men, would be guaranteed the unalienable rights of life, liberty, and the pursuit of happiness.

34 "Martin Luther King Jr. I Have a Dream Speech." *American Rhetoric*, 20 Aug, 2020, www.americanrhetoric.com/speeches/mlkihaveadream.htm.

It is obvious today that America has defaulted on this promissory note insofar as her citizens of color are concerned. Instead of honoring this sacred obligation, America has given the Negro people a bad check, a check which has come back marked "insufficient funds." But we refuse to believe that the bank of justice is bankrupt. We refuse to believe that there are insufficient funds in the great vaults of opportunity of this nation. So we have come to cash this check—a check that will give us upon demand the riches of freedom and the security of justice.

We have also come to this hallowed spot to remind America of the fierce urgency of now. This is no time to engage in the luxury of cooling off or to take the tranquilizing drug of gradualism. Now is the time to make real the promises of democracy. Now is the time to rise from the dark and desolate valley of segregation to the sunlit path of racial justice. Now is the time to lift our nation from the quick sands of racial injustice to the solid rock of brotherhood. Now is the time to make justice a reality for all of God's children.

It would be fatal for the nation to overlook the urgency of the moment. This sweltering summer of the Negro's legitimate discontent will not pass until there is an invigorating autumn of freedom and equality. Nineteen sixty-three is not an end, but a beginning. Those who hope that the Negro needed to blow off steam and will now be content will have a rude awakening if the nation returns to business as usual. There will be neither rest nor tranquility in America until the Negro is granted his citizenship rights. The whirlwinds of revolt will continue to shake the foundations of our nation until the bright day of justice emerges.

But there is something that I must say to my people who stand on the warm threshold which leads into the palace of justice. In the process of gaining our rightful place we must not be guilty of wrongful deeds. Let us not seek to satisfy our thirst for freedom by drinking from the cup of bitterness and hatred.

We must forever conduct our struggle on the high plane of dignity and discipline **[assonance]**. We must not allow our creative protest to degenerate into physical violence. Again and again we must rise to the majestic heights of meeting physical force with soul force. The marvelous new militancy which has engulfed the Negro community must not lead us to a distrust of all white people, for many of our white brothers, as evidenced by their presence here today, have come to realize that their destiny is tied up with our destiny. They have come to realize that their freedom is inextricably bound to our freedom. We cannot walk alone.

As we walk, we must make the pledge that we shall always march ahead. We cannot turn back. There are those who are asking the devotees of civil rights, "When will you be satisfied?" **[hypophora]** We can never be satisfied as long as the Negro is the victim of the unspeakable horrors of police brutality. We can never be satisfied, as long as our bodies, heavy with the fatigue of travel, cannot gain lodging in the motels of the highways and the hotels of the cities. We cannot be satisfied as long as the Negro's basic mobility is from a smaller ghetto to a larger one. We can never be satisfied as long as our children are stripped of their selfhood and robbed of their dignity by signs stating "For Whites Only". We cannot be satisfied as long as a Negro in Mississippi cannot vote and a Negro in New York believes he has nothing for which to vote. No, no, we are not satisfied, and we will not be satisfied until justice rolls down like waters and righteousness like a mighty stream **[simile]**.

I am not unmindful that some of you have come here out of great trials and tribulations. Some of you have come fresh from narrow jail cells. Some of you have come from areas where your quest for freedom left you battered by the storms of persecution and staggered by the winds of police brutality.

You have been the veterans of creative suffering. Continue to work with the faith that unearned suffering is redemptive.

Go back to Mississippi, go back to Alabama, go back to South Carolina, go back to Georgia, go back to Louisiana **[asyndeton]**, go back to the slums and ghettos of our northern cities, knowing that somehow this situation can and will be changed. Let us not wallow in the valley of despair.

I say to you today, my friends, so even though we face the difficulties of today and tomorrow, I still have a dream. It is a dream deeply rooted in the American dream.

I have a dream **[anaphora]** that one day this nation will rise up and live out the true meaning of its creed: "We hold these truths to be self-evident: that all men are created equal."

I have a dream that one day on the red hills of Georgia the sons of former slaves and the sons of former slave owners will be able to sit down together at the table of brotherhood.

I have a dream that one day even the state of Mississippi, a state sweltering with the heat of injustice **[metaphor]**, sweltering with the heat of oppression, will be transformed into an oasis of freedom and justice.

I have a dream that my four little children will one day live in a nation where they will not be judged by the color of their skin but by the content of their character **[alliteration].**

I have a dream today.

I have a dream that one day, down in Alabama, with its vicious racists, with its governor having his lips dripping with the words of interposition and nullification; one day right there in Alabama, little black boys and black girls will be able to join hands with little white boys and white girls as sisters and brothers.

I have a dream today.

I have a dream that one day every valley shall be exalted, every hill and mountain shall be made low, the rough places will be made plain, and the crooked places will be made straight, and the glory of the Lord shall be revealed, and all flesh shall see it together.

This is our hope. This is the faith that I go back to the South with. With this faith we will be able to hew out of the mountain of despair a stone of hope. With this faith we will be able to transform the jangling discords of our nation into a beautiful symphony of brotherhood. With this faith we will be able to work together, to pray together, to struggle together, to go to jail together, to stand up for freedom together, knowing that we will be free one day.

This will be the day when all of God's children will be able to sing with a new meaning, "My country, 'tis of thee, sweet land of liberty, of thee I sing. Land where my fathers died, land of the pilgrim's pride, from every mountainside, let freedom ring."

And if America is to be a great nation this must become true. So let freedom ring from the prodigious hilltops of New Hampshire. Let freedom ring from the mighty mountains of New York. Let freedom ring from the heightening Alleghenies of Pennsylvania!

Let freedom ring from the snowcapped Rockies of Colorado!

Let freedom ring from the curvaceous slopes of California!

But not only that; let freedom ring from Stone Mountain of Georgia!

Let freedom ring from Lookout Mountain of Tennessee!

Let freedom ring from every hill and molehill of Mississippi. From every mountainside, let freedom ring.

And when this happens, when we allow freedom to ring, when we let it ring from every village and every hamlet, from every state and every city, we will be able to speed up that day when all of God's children, black men and white men, Jews and Gentiles, Protestants and Catholics, will be able to join hands and sing in the words of the old Negro spiritual, "Free at last! Free at last! Thank God Almighty, we are free at last!"

SEAL OF THE PRESIDENT OF THE UNITED STATES

SPEECH 2: PRESIDENT JOHN F. KENNEDY[35]

Inaugural Address

January 20, 1961

Vice President Johnson, Mr. Speaker, Mr. Chief Justice, President Eisenhower, Vice President Nixon, President Truman, reverend clergy, fellow citizens:

We observe today not a victory of party, but a celebration of freedom—symbolizing an end, as well as a beginning—signifying renewal, as well as change. For I have sworn before you and Almighty God the same solemn oath **[alliteration]** our forebears prescribed nearly a century and three-quarters ago.

The world is very different now. For man holds in his mortal hands the power to abolish all forms of human poverty and all forms of human life. And yet the same revolutionary beliefs for which our forebears fought are still at issue around the globe—the belief that the rights of man come not from the generosity of the state, but from the hand of God.

We dare not forget today that we are the heirs of that first revolution. Let the word go forth from this time and place, to friend and foe alike, that the torch has been passed to a new generation of Americans—born in this century, tempered by war, disciplined by a hard and bitter peace, proud of our ancient heritage, and unwilling to witness or permit the slow undoing of those human rights to which this nation has always been committed, and to which we are committed today at home and around the world.

---

35 "John Fitzgerald Kennedy, Inaugural Address (20 January 1961)" *Voices of Democracy*, 5 July 2016, http://voicesofdemocracy.umd.edu/kennedy-inaugural-address-speech-text/.

Let every nation know, whether it wishes us well or ill, that we shall pay any price, bear any burden, meet any hardship, support any friend, oppose any foe, to assure the survival and the success of liberty.

This much we pledge—and more.

To those old allies whose cultural and spiritual origins we share, we pledge the loyalty of faithful friends. United there is little we cannot do in a host of cooperative ventures. Divided there is little we can do—for we dare not meet a powerful challenge at odds and split asunder.

To those new states whom we welcome to the ranks of the free, we pledge our word that one form of colonial control shall not have passed away merely to be replaced by a far more iron tyranny. We shall not always expect to find them supporting our view. But we shall always hope to find them strongly supporting their own freedom—and to remember that, in the past, those who foolishly sought power by riding the back of the tiger ended up inside.

To those **[anaphora]** people in the huts and villages of half the globe struggling to break the bonds of mass misery, we pledge our best efforts to help them help themselves, for whatever period is required—not because the Communists may be doing it, not because we seek their votes, but because it is right. If a free society cannot help the many who are poor, it cannot save the few who are rich.

To our sister republics south of our border, we offer a special pledge: to convert our good words into good deeds, in a new alliance for progress, to assist free men and free governments in casting off the chains of poverty **[metaphor]**. But this peaceful revolution of hope cannot become the prey of hostile powers. Let all our neighbors know that we shall join with them to oppose aggression or subversion anywhere in the Americas. And let every other power know that this hemisphere intends to remain the master of its own house.

To that world assembly of sovereign states, the United Nations, our last best hope in an age where the instruments of war have far outpaced the instruments of peace, we renew our pledge of support—to prevent it from becoming merely a forum for invective, to strengthen its shield of the new and the weak, and to enlarge the area in which its writ may run.

Finally, to those nations who would make themselves our adversary, we offer not a pledge but a request: that both sides begin anew the quest for peace, before the dark powers of destruction unleashed by science engulf all humanity in planned or accidental self-destruction.

We dare not tempt them with weakness. For only when our arms are sufficient beyond doubt can we be certain beyond doubt that they will never be employed.

But neither can two great and powerful groups of nations take comfort from our present course—both sides overburdened by the cost of modern weapons, both rightly alarmed by the steady spread of the deadly atom, yet both racing to alter that uncertain balance of terror that stays the hand of mankind's final war.

So let us begin anew—remembering on both sides that civility is not a sign of weakness, and sincerity is always subject to proof. Let us never negotiate out of fear, but let us never fear to negotiate.

Let both sides explore what problems unite us instead of belaboring those problems which divide us.

Let both sides, for the first time, formulate serious and precise proposals for the inspection and control of arms, and bring the absolute power to destroy other nations under the absolute control of all nations.

Let both sides seek to invoke the wonders of science instead of its terrors. Together let us explore the stars, conquer the deserts, eradicate disease, tap the ocean depths, and encourage the arts and commerce.

Let both sides unite to heed, in all corners of the Earth, the command of Isaiah—to "undo the heavy burdens, and [to] let the oppressed go free."

And, if a beachhead of cooperation **[anaphora]** may push back the jungle of suspicion, let both sides join in creating a new endeavor—not a new balance of power, but a new world of law—where the strong are just, and the weak secure, and the peace preserved.

All this will not be finished in the first one hundred days. Nor will it be finished in the first one thousand days; nor in the life of this Administration; nor even perhaps in our lifetime on this planet. But let us begin.

In your hands, my fellow citizens, more than mine, will rest the final success or failure of our course. Since this country was founded, each generation of Americans has been summoned to give testimony to its national loyalty. The graves of young Americans who answered the call to service surround the globe.

Now the trumpet summons us again—not as a call to bear arms, though arms we need—not as a call to battle, though embattled we are—but a call to bear the burden of a long twilight struggle, year in and year out, "rejoicing in hope; patient in tribulation," a struggle against the common enemies of man: tyranny, poverty, disease, **[triad]** and war itself.

Can we forge against these enemies a grand and global alliance, North and South, East and West, that can assure a more fruitful life for all mankind? Will you join in that historic effort? **[hypophora]**

In the long history of the world, only a few generations have been granted the role of defending freedom in its hour of maximum danger. I do not shrink from this responsibility—I welcome it. I do not believe that any of us would exchange places with any other people or any other generation.

The energy, the faith, the devotion **[asyndeton]** which we bring to this endeavor will light our country and all who serve it. And the glow from that fire can truly light the world.

And so, my fellow Americans, ask not what your country can do for you; ask what you can do for your country. **[chiasmus]**

My fellow citizens of the world, ask not what America will do for you, but what together we can do for the freedom of man.

Finally, whether you are citizens of America or citizens of the world, ask of us here the same high standards of strength and sacrifice **[alliteration]** which we ask of you.

With a good conscience our only sure reward, with history the final judge of our deeds, let us go forth to lead the land we love **[alliteration]**, asking His blessing and His help, but knowing that here on Earth God's work must truly be our own.

Works Cited

Ali, Iftikhar. "They thought bullets will silence us, but they failed : Malala on Malala Day at UN." myglobalcommunityday, *WordPress*, 13 Jul. 2013, https://myglobalcommunitytoday.wordpress.com/2013/07/13/they-thought-bullets-will-silence-us-but-they-failed-malala-on-malala-day-at-un/.

"America Meets a Lot. An Analysis of Meeting Length, Frequency and Cost." *Attentiv*, 23 Sept. 2015, attentiv.com/america-meets-a-lot/.

Astramskas, David. "Storytime: Team USA trainer tells a story about Kobe's insane work ethic."*Ballislife.com*, 6 Mar. 2014, https://ballislife.com/storytime-team-usa-trainer-kobe/.

Ayres, Joe, and Tim Hopf. "Visualization: Reducing speech anxiety and enhancing performance." *Communication Reports* 5.1 (1992): 1-10.

Baker, Peter. "Tales of Totus, the President's Teleprompter." The Caucus, *The New York Times*, 29 Mar. 2009, http://thecaucus.blogs.nytimes.com/2009/03/25/tales-of-totus-the-presidents-teleprompter/.

Bradberry, Travis. "Multitasking Damages Your Brain And Career, New Studies Suggest." *Forbes*, Forbes Magazine, 20 Jan. 2015, www.forbes.com/sites/travisbradberry/2014/10/08/multitasking-damages-your-brain-and-career-new-studies-suggest/.

Casserly, Meghan. "10 Body Language Tics That Could Cost You The Interview—And The Job." *Forbes*, Forbes Magazine, 26 Mar. 2014, www.forbes.com/sites/meghancasserly/2012/09/26/10-body-language-tics-that-could-cost-you-the-interview-and-the-job/.

Cook, Susan Wagner, et al. "Gesturing Makes Memories That Last." *Journal of Memory and Language*, U.S. National Library of Medicine, Nov. 2010, www.ncbi.nlm.nih.gov/pmc/articles/PMC3124384/.

Cuddy, Amy J.C., Wilmuth, Caroline A., and Carney, Dana R. "The Benefit of Power Posing Before a High-Stakes Social Evaluation." Harvard Business School Working Paper, No. 13-027, September 2012.

WORKS CITED

Dag, O. "George Orwell." *George Orwell: Politics and the English Language*, www.orwell.ru/library/essays/politics/english/e_polit/.

"Death to PowerPoint!" *Bloomberg.com*, Bloomberg, 30 Aug. 2012, www .bloomberg.com/news/articles/2012-08-30/death-to-powerpoint.

"George Orwell." *Biography.com*, A&E Networks Television, 16 Jan. 2020, www .biography.com/writer/george-orwell.

Hitti, Miranda. "Can You Smell Through Your Mouth?" *WebMD*, WebMD, 17 Aug. 2005, www.webmd.com/brain/news/20050817/can-you-smell -through-your-mouth.

"John Fitzgerald Kennedy, Inaugural Address (20 January 1961)." *Voices of Democracy*, 5 July 2016, http://voicesofdemocracy.umd.edu/kennedy -inaugural-address-speech-text/.

"Kennedy-Nixon Debates." *History.com*, A&E Television Networks, 24 Nov. 2009, www.history.com/this-day-in-history/first-kennedy-nixon-debate.

Malcolm, Andrew. "Happy Birthday, Gettysburg Address." Hot Air, 20 Nov. 2010, https://hotair.com/archives/latimestot/2010/11/20/happy -birthday-gettysburg-address/.

"Martin Luther King Jr. I Have a Dream Speech." *American Rhetoric*, 20 Aug. 2020, www.americanrhetoric.com/speeches/mlkihaveadream.htm.

McCoy, Sean. "How to Get Sponsored in Outdoor Sports: A Pro Athlete Shares His Insights." *GearJunkie*, 22 Aug. 2020, gearjunkie.com/how-to -get-sponsored-outdoor-sports-athlete.

McSpadden, Kevin. "Science: You Now Have a Shorter Attention Span Than a Goldfish." *Time*, Time, 14 May 2015, time.com/3858309/attention -spans-goldfish/.

Miller, Tim. "What Is Ujjayi?" *Yoga Journal*, 28 Aug. 2007, www.yogajournal .com/practice/what-is-ujjayi.

The National Archives. "Churchill's Call for Brevity." *The National Archives Blog*, The National Archives, 17 Oct. 2013, blog.nationalarchives.gov.uk /churchills-call-for-brevity/.

O'Neill, Megan. "Longest YouTube Video Ever Will Take You 23 Days To Watch." *Adweek*, Adweek, 28 July 2011, www.adweek.com/digital/longest-youtube-video/.

"Reframing Stress: Stage Fright Can Be Your Friend." *Association for Psychological Science - APS*, 8 Apr. 2013, www.psychologicalscience.org/news/releases/reframing-stress-stage-fright-can-be-your-friend.html.

Romano, N.C., and J.F. Nunamaker. "Meeting Analysis: Findings from Research and Practice." *Proceedings of the 34th Annual Hawaii International Conference on System Sciences*, 2001, https://doi.org/10.1109/hicss.2001.926253.

Salass, Nader. "Malala Day At UN: Teen Activist Shot By Taliban Said 10 Moving Things That Gave Us Goosebumps (VIDEO)." *HuffPost*, 6 Dec. 2016, www.huffpost.com/entry/malala-day-at-un_n_3586266.

Savitsky, Kenneth, and Thomas Gilovich. "The Illusion of Transparency and the Alleviation of Speech Anxiety." *Journal of Experimental Social Psychology*, vol. 39, no. 6, 2003, pp. 618–625, https://doi.org/10.1016/s0022-1031(03)00056-8.

"The Scaffolding of Rhetoric," The International Churchill Society, https://winstonchurchill.org/publications/finest-hour/finest-hour-094/the-scaffolding-of-rhetoric-2/.

Schroeder, Juliana, and Nicholas Epley. "The Sound of Intellect." *Psychological Science*, vol. 26, no. 6, 2015, pp. 877–891, https://doi.org/10.1177/0956797615572906.

Slepian, Michael L., et al. "The Cognitive Consequences of Formal Clothing." *Social Psychological and Personality Science*, vol. 6, no. 6, 2015, pp. 661–668, https://doi.org/10.1177/1948550615579462.

"William Bourke Cockran." Wikipedia, Wikimedia Foundation, 31 Dec. 2020, http:/en.wikipedia.org/wiki/William_Bourke_Cockran.

About the Oratory Project

The Oratory Project (T.O.P.) is a mission-based service that delivers customized, proprietary workshops to enhance the communication skills of young adults. These workshops focus on empowerment and professional growth.

The Oratory Project workshops are strictly offered through sponsoring partner organizations and are 100% free for participants. If your organization is interested in sponsoring an Oratory Project workshop, please visit oratoryproject.org.

College Scholarship Leadership Access Program

Our Mission is College Access For All

The College Scholarship Leadership Access Program (CSLAP) believes every student can attend and graduate from college. Based in the Rio Grande Valley, CSLAP is a 501(c)(3) nonprofit that teaches college access classes during the instructional day, after school, and over the summer. CSLAP also provides one-on-one college coaching sessions, awards scholarships, and partners with community organizations to expand opportunities for students from all backgrounds.

About the Author

Matt Eventoff is a communication and messaging strategist. He helps leaders succeed, organizations grow and executives gain the necessary confidence to present authentically, passionately and confidently.

He has served as a strategic advisor and high-stakes communications trainer for leading multinational organizations and brands, the U.S. Department of State, U.S. Department of Defense, internationally recognized personalities and executives from myriad industries.

Matt has trained senior executives on-site in over 90 countries, and has delivered workshops on effective communication, intercultural communication, executive presence and crisis communication on six continents.

He has prepared speakers to present at nearly every event, ranging from earnings calls and board meetings to media appearances to appearances at TED, the World Economic Forum (Davos), the United Nations, CES, the Aspen Ideas festival and before legislative bodies on four continents.

He has lectured on communication and public speaking topics at Princeton University, University of Pennsylvania, University of Texas, Notre Dame, University of Miami School of Law and numerous other colleges and universities both in the United States and overseas. He was previously an adjunct professor in the Rutgers University Business School Executive MBA program.

Matt was selected to participate in the State Department's Speaker Specialist Program, and is regularly cited by leading publications and news outlets on issues related to communication.

In addition, he operates The Oratory Project, which provides free public speaking training and workshops to at-risk young adults and served as the professional advisor to the Princeton University student organization Speak with Style for nearly a decade.

Matt is the author of *Oratore: The Art of Communication, It Really Is As Simple As ABC: What Leaders Can Learn From Masterful Orators,* and *The Oratory Project* (September 2023 release) and is the co-author of *History's Greatest Leaders and You.*

Additionally, he is the author of *Speak Fearlessly,* a graphic novel, and the co-author of *Speechless,* an illustrated picture book. These are the first in a series of free children's books aimed to help children overcome the fear of public speaking. *Speak Fearlessly, Speechless* and other new titles are offered for free to at-risk children and young adults in multiple languages.

Matt received his Bachelor's degree from the University of Maryland and his Master's degree from the University of Pennsylvania.

Made in the USA
Middletown, DE
30 October 2024

63575731R00142